fair isle style

20 fresh designs for a classic technique

mary jane mucklestone

INTERWEAVE
interweave.com

Editor Ann Budd
Technical Editor Lori Gayle
Photographer (beauty) Chris Vaccaro
Photographer (swatches) Joe Coca
Photo Stylist Mary Jane Mucklestone
Hair and Makeup Cheyenne Timperio
Cover and Interior Designer Julia Boyles
Illustrator Kathie Kelleher
Production Katherine Jackson

Interweave Press LLC
A division of F+W Media, Inc.
201 East Fourth Street
Loveland, CO 80537
interweave.com

Manufactured in China by RR Donnelley Shenzhen

Library of Congress Cataloging-in-Publication Data

Mucklestone, Mary Jane.
Fair Isle style : 20 fresh designs for a classic technique /
Mary Jane Mucklestone.
        pages cm
Includes bibliographical references and index.
ISBN 978-1-59668-899-5 (pbk.)
ISBN 978-1-59668-926-8 (PDF)
1. Knitting—Patterns. 2. Knitting—Scotland—Fair Isle—
Patterns. I. Title.
TT819.G72M76 2013
746.43'2--dc23
2012050665

10 9 8 7 6 5 4 3 2 1

Acknowledgments

I'd like to express my gratitude to the talented designers whose imaginative takes on Fair Isle knitting appear in this book: Elinor Brown, Cheryl Burke, Nancy Bush, Kat Coyle, Jane Dupuis, Norah Gaughan, Lucinda Guy, Carrie Bostick Hoge, Gudrun Johnston, Mags Kandis, Kirsten Kapur, Courtney Kelly, Kate Gagnon Osborn, Lisa Shroyer, Elli Stubenrauch, and Ysolda Teague. You've all contributed to the continued life of and contemporary take on an old and venerable tradition. I feel lucky to call you talented women my friends and colleagues.

Thanks must also be extended to the yarn companies without whose generous yarn contributions this book would not have been possible: Berroco, Brooklyn Tweed, Brown Sheep Company, Cascade Yarns, Classic Elite Yarns, Elemental Affects, Green Mountain Spinnery, Harrisville Designs, Jamieson & Smith, Simply Shetland/Jamieson's of Shetland, St-Denis, Quince and Company, Sunday Knits Yarns, Kelbourne Woolens/ The Fibre Company, and Tutto Santa Fe/Isager Yarns. Your beautiful yarns were often the inspiration for the resulting designs.

Many thanks to Lori Gayle for her thoughtful and diligent technical editing. Tech editors are the unsung heroes of the industry, and Lori is deserving of an opera.

Special thanks to Ann Budd, whose belief in and guidance along the way made the entire project possible.

Many thanks to Chris Vacarro for his stellar photographs, can-do attitude, and willingness to squeeze this book into his busy schedule at the eleventh hour. The same goes for hair and makeup artist Cheyenne Timperio, whose inspired work and great personality ensure even the most difficult shoot is a pleasure! To our models, Sophie Scott, Sunny Hitt, Kim Riposta, and Teal, thanks for your cheerful willingness to oblige our every whim— your beautiful presence allowed the designers' work to shine. Thanks to Larissa Davis for signing on at the last moment and becoming the backbone of our Maine team. Your help was invaluable and much appreciated. Kristin Flynn of Over the Rainbow Yarns of Rockland, Maine, deserves special recognition for the unseen tasks she did, including making sure we all got to eat! And thanks to Mim Bird, owner of Over the Rainbow Yarns, for lending Kristin to us for the day.

Thanks also go to Beloin's Motel and Costal Mountain Land Trust, both of Camden, Maine, and to Belfast Bay Inn of Belfast, Maine, for allowing us access to your gorgeous seaside and sea-view properties.

Finally, thanks to my family who may not always understand what I'm talking about, but will nod politely and offer me encouragement. Thanks for helping me when I let the daily tasks of family living drift by the wayside and never letting me feel that I wasn't doing enough. I love you all!

Contents

6 Inspiration from Fair Isle

8 Kulli Cowl Ysolda Teague

12 Lumesadu Gloves Nancy Bush

20 Morroless Socks Mary Jane Mucklestone

26 Mirry-Dancers Yoked Pullover
Cheryl Burke

34 Ketlin Skirt Kat Coyle

40 Mushroom Kelliemuffs
SpillyJane, a.k.a. Jane Dupuis

44 Mirknin Hat and Scarf Elinor Brown

48 Bressay Dress Gudrun Johnston

58 Peerie Weerie Booties
Carrie Bostick Hoge

62 Hap-Lapghan Kirsten Kapur

68 Babsie Bird Lucinda Guy

76 Valenzi Cardigan Mary Jane Mucklestone

84 Fara Raglan Courtney Kelley

94 Mud Cloth Bag Mags Kandis

98 Mareel Shrug Norah Gaughan

106 Squirrel-in-the-Woods Mittens
Elli Stubenrauch

112 Mayflooer Mittens
Elli Stubenrauch

118 Scandi Sukkalegs
Kate Gagnon Osborn

122 Reeva Hat Lisa Shroyer

126 Design Notebook

146 Glossary of Terms and Techniques

155 Contributing Designers

157 Bibliography

158 Sources for Yarn

159 Index

Inspiration from Fair Isle

Originating in Fair Isle, a tiny island in the northernmost archipelago (Shetland) of the British Isles, Fair Isle knitting has been produced continuously for two hundred years or more. As popular today as ever, Fair Isle knits are routinely present on the high-fashion runways of Paris and New York. This seemingly complex colorwork knitting is surprisingly simple to create and great fun for the knitter.

True Fair Isle knitting never uses more than two colors in any row, yet it achieves fantastic color effects from elegantly subtle shadings to wild riots of color. If you're new to the technique, begin with a simple project that uses just a touch of color—a two-color band that encircles a cowl, for example—and work your way up to a more complex color arrangement that includes many colors in the same pattern motif. Whatever your wish, these patterns offer enticing choices for every skill level.

Fair Isle Style is a collection of twenty patterns from seventeen talented and inventive knitwear designers, each of whom has used traditional Fair Isle knitting as a point of departure to create something unique, be it a dress, skirt, shrug, sweater, mitten, hat, or even a delightful stuffed toy! Every design offers an individual lesson in inspiration, technique application, and, of course, style. As a collection, the patterns will give you new ways to think about Fair Isle knitting and provide you with ideas and inspiration for your own inventions.

After you have taken in the twenty designs, turn to the Design Notebook where you'll find a discussion of the basics of Fair Isle knitting, including holding and managing two yarns, dealing with floats, and combining colors successfully. The seemingly terrifying technique of steeking is also clearly explained and will put your fears to rest.

Don't worry if you're new to Fair Isle knitting. At the end of the book you'll find a glossary of terms and techniques that includes illustrated instructions for all the specific techniques mentioned in the projects. Along with easy-to-follow directions and clear illustrations in the project and design chapters, this glossary will provide all the help you need to successfully complete any project in this book.

What's in a Name?

The names of many of the garments in this book contain words from Shetland dialect, a language that is very much alive today. There are several online sources to learn more about Shetland dialect, and it is from these sites that the words were mined. Apologies if any words are misused.

hap (n): handknitted shawl (Hap-Lapghan, page 62).

kelliemuff (n): a mitt (Mushroom Kelliemuffs, page 40).

ketlin (n): kitten (Ketlin Skirt, page 34).

kulli (n): cowl (Kulli Cowl, page 8).

mareel (n): phosphorescence in the sea at twilight or dark, e.g., from oar tips (Mareel Shrug, page 98).

mayflooer (n): Primula, a flower that blooms in May (Mayflooer Mittens, page 112).

mirknin (n): dusk, twilight (Mirknin Hat and Scarf, page 44).

mirry-dancers (n): northern lights, aurora borealis (Mirry-Dancers Yoked Pullover, page 26).

morroless (adj): unmatched, odd (Morroless Socks, page 20).

peerie weerie (adj): very, very small (Peerie Weerie Booties, page 58).

sukkalegs (n): stockings without feet (Scandi Sukkalegs, page 118).

valenzi (n): violent gale (Valenzi Cardigan, page 76).

SOURCES

Shetland for Wirds
shetlanddialect.org.uk/dictionary
You can listen to the spoken language here.

Angus, James Stout. *A Glossary of the Shetland Dialect*. 1914. Available online at: http://archive.org/details/cu31924026538979.

inspiration from fair isle

Kulli Cowl

DESIGNED BY YSOLDA TEAGUE

A cowl makes a wonderful introduction to Fair Isle knitting, and the one **Ysolda Teague** designed is interesting enough to enchant even experienced knitters. Bands of solid-color garter stitch cleverly worked in the round alternate with a series of sweet peerie (small) patterns for a deceptively complicated impression of color and texture. To keep the piece light and airy, Ysolda chose a fingering-weight alpaca that she worked at a fairly loose gauge. She followed a traditional color palette of golden yellow that contrasts with rich madder red paired with a pale natural gray, but the overall effect is strictly modern.

FINISHED SIZE

About 34" (86.5 cm) circumference and 9" (23 cm) tall, blocked.

YARN

Laceweight (#0 Lace).

Shown here: Isager Alpaca 1 (100% baby alpaca; 437 yd [400 m]/50 g): #3 old gold (MC), #21 red (CC1), and #2s light natural gray (CC2), 1 ball each.

NEEDLES

Single-color rnds: size U.S. 2 (2.75 mm): 24" (60 cm) circular (cir).

Fair Isle rnds: size U.S. 3 (3.25 mm): 24" (60 cm) cir.

Adjust needle size if necessary to obtain the correct gauge.

NOTIONS

Stitch marker (m); tapestry needle.

GAUGE

28 sts and 56 rnds = 4" (10 cm) in garter stitch, worked in rnds with smaller needle, after blocking.

stitch guide

Garter Stitch in Rounds without Purling

Note: In this pattern, "other strand" refers to the strand of yarn not used for the previous round. On the very first round, you may use either strand.

Rnd 1: With RS facing, pick up the other strand of MC, knit to end of rnd, then turn piece so WS is facing, drop yarn.

Rnd 2: With WS facing, pick up other strand of MC and knit to end of rnd, turn piece so RS is facing, drop yarn.

Rep Rnds 1 and 2 for pattern.

notes

○ All solid and charted rounds using CC1 and CC2 are worked in stockinette in the round with the RS of the work always facing you.

○ If you are working from a center-pull ball of MC, take the two strands used for working garter stitch in the round without purling (see above) from the inside and outside of the same ball. Allow the center-pull ball to dangle from the work to untwist strands when necessary.

Cowl

With CC1 and CC2 held tog and smaller needle, CO 240 sts. Cut yarns. With RS facing, join 2 strands of MC, then drop 1 strand.

Rnd 1: Working each double CO st as a single st, work Rnd 1 of garter st in rnds without purling (see Stitch Guide), turn work so WS is facing, place marker (pm), and join for working in rnds.

Rnds 2–12: Work Rnd 2 of garter st in rnds, then rep Rnds 1 and 2 five more times.

Cut both strands of MC.

Rnd 13: Join CC1 and knit 1 rnd.

Rnds 14–18: Change to larger needle. Join CC2 and work Rnds 1–5 of Chart A.

Cut CC2.

Rnd 19: Change to smaller needle. Knit 1 rnd with CC1.

Cut yarn.

Rnds 20–33: Join 2 strands of MC. Work Rnds 1 and 2 of garter st in rnds 7 times.

Cut both strands of MC.

Rnd 34: Join CC2 and knit 1 rnd.

Rnds 35–41: Change to larger needle. Join CC1 and work Rnds 1–7 of Chart B.

Cut CC1.

Rnd 42: Change to smaller needle. Knit 1 rnd with CC2.

Cut yarn.

Rnds 43–56: Join 2 strands of MC. Work Rnds 1 and 2 of garter st in rnds 7 times.

Cut both strands of MC.

Rnd 57: Join CC1 and knit 1 rnd.

Rnds 58–66: Change to larger needle. Join CC2 and work Rnds 1–9 of Chart C.

Cut CC2.

Rnd 67: Change to smaller needle. Knit 1 rnd with CC1.

Cut yarn.

Rnds 68–81: Join 2 strands of MC. Work Rnds 1 and 2 of garter st in rnds 7 times.

Cut both strands of MC.

Rnd 82: Join CC2 and knit 1 rnd.

Rnds 83–89: Change to larger needle. Join CC1 and work Rnds 1–7 of Chart D.

Cut CC1.

Rnd 90: Change to smaller needle. Knit 1 rnd with CC2.

Cut yarn.

Rnds 91–104: Join 2 strands of MC. Work Rnds 1 and 2 of garter st in rnds 7 times.

Cut both strands of MC.

Rnd 105: Join CC1 and knit 1 rnd.

Rnds 106–110: Change to larger needle. Join CC2 and work Rnds 1–5 of Chart E.

Cut CC2.

Rnd 111: Change to smaller needle. Knit 1 rnd with CC1.

Cut yarn.

Rnds 112–121: Join 2 strands of MC. Work Rnds 1 and 2 of garter st in rnds 5 times.

Cut both strands of MC.

With CC1 and CC2 held tog, knit 1 rnd.

BO all sts.

Finishing

Weave in loose ends. Block to measurements.

Chart A

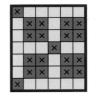

5
3
1

6-st repeat

Chart B

7
5
3
1

6-st repeat

Chart C

9
7
5
3
1

12-st repeat

Chart D

7
5
3
1

6-st repeat

Chart E

5
3
1

8-st repeat

× CC1

CC2

pattern repeat

Lumesadu Gloves

DESIGNED BY NANCY BUSH

Scholars believe the inspiration for what we think of as typical Fair Isle patterns, specifically the classic OXO pattern, came from the Baltic region. Many of the patterns on knitted mittens and gloves in the Estonian knitting tradition were derived from weaving patterns used in weaving belts, which almost always have X and O figured patterns. Following the tradition for Estonian gloves, **Nancy Bush's** version features a limited color palette for the pattern stitches against a solid background. The name, *lumesadu,* is the Estonian word for "snowfall."

FINISHED SIZE
About 8" (20.5 cm) hand circumference and 9" (23 cm) from CO to tip of longest finger, after blocking.

YARN
Fingering weight (#1 Super Fine).

Shown here: Elemental Affects North American Shetland (100% wool; 118 yd [108 m]/1 oz [28.4 g]): musket (MC; gray), 2 skeins; #0005 Mediterranean night (A; dark green), #0037 sea foam (B; light teal), #0012 berry (C; dark rose), and #0019 pretty pink streak (D), 1 skein each.

NEEDLES
Ribbing: size U.S. 0 (2 mm): set of 5 double-pointed (dpn).

Hand, fingers, and thumb: size 2 (2.75 mm): set of 5 dpn.

Adjust needle size if necessary to obtain the correct gauge.

NOTIONS
Smooth cotton waste yarn; tapestry needle.

GAUGE
15 sts and 15 rnds = 2" (10 cm) in charted pattern on larger needles, worked in rnds, before blocking.

14 sts and 17 rnds = 2" (10 cm) in charted pattern on larger needles, worked in rnds, after blocking.

Cuff and Lower Hand (same for right and left gloves)

With MC, smaller needles, and using the double-start method (see Glossary), CO 56 sts. Divide sts evenly on 4 dpn (14 sts on each needle). Join for working in rnds, being careful not to twist sts. The CO tails mark the end of the rnd. Continue with single strand (yarn attached to the ball).

Knit 1 rnd, then purl 1 rnd.

Rib rnd: *K2, p2; rep from * to end.

Rep the rib rnd until piece measures 2¼" (5.5 cm) from CO.

Change to larger needles.

Next rnd: Work Rnd 1 of Estonian Star chart, working 28-st patt rep twice around.

Work Rnds 2–19 of chart as established.

Continue for right or left hand as follows.

Right Hand

Rnds begin at little-finger side of the hand, at start of back-of-hand sts.

Next rnd: (thumb placement, Rnd 20 of chart) Keeping in patt, work all 28 back-of-hand sts on Needle 1 and Needle 2; on Needle 3, work first 12 sts then place these 12 sts onto a length of smooth cotton waste yarn, work last 2 sts of Needle 3; work 14 sts of Needle 4 to end of rnd.

Next rnd: (Rnd 21 of chart) Work in patt to thumb gap of previous rnd, use the backward-loop method (see

Glossary) to CO 12 sts in chart patt across the gap, work in patt to end—still 56 sts.

Work Rnds 22–34 of chart—piece measures about 1¾" (4.5 cm) from thumb opening.

Try on glove to be sure it reaches to the base of your index and middle fingers. If not, work additional rnds with MC until hand is desired length.

Finger Set-Up

Move the first st from Needle 1 onto the end of Needle 4, then move the last st from Needle 2 onto the beg of Needle 3—13 sts each on Needle 1 and Needle 2, 15 sts each on Needle 3 and Needle 4. Fingers and thumb are worked in St st with MC.

Estonian Star

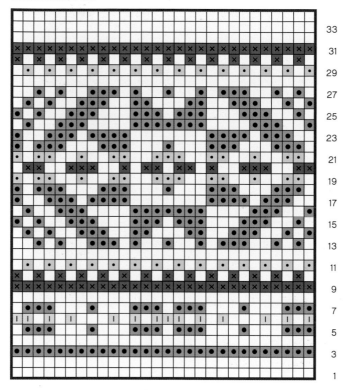

33
31
29
27
25
23
21
19
17
15
13
11
9
7
5
3
1

28-st repeat

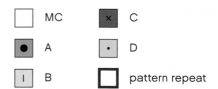

	MC			C
●	A	•		D
I	B			pattern repeat

INDEX FINGER

Set-up rnd: On Needle 1, k13; on Needle 2, knit the first 4 sts, place the last 17 sts worked onto cotton waste-yarn holder, then knit the rem 9 sts of Needle 2; with an empty needle, knit the first 9 sts of Needle 3, use the backward-loop method to CO 5 sts, then place rem 6 sts of Needle 3 and all 15 sts of Needle 4 onto other end of same waste-yarn holder—23 sts rem for index finger; 38 sts on holder.

Arrange sts as evenly as possible onto 3 dpn and join for working in rnds. Work even in St st until finger measures about 2½" (6.5 cm) from joining rnd or reaches the middle of the wearer's fingernail.

Next rnd: *K1, k2tog, rep from * to last 2 sts, k2—16 sts rem.

Next rnd: Knit.

Next rnd: [K2tog] 8 times—8 sts rem.

Cut yarn, leaving an 8" (20.5 cm) tail. Thread tail on a tapestry needle, draw through rem sts, pull tight to close hole, and fasten off on WS.

MIDDLE FINGER

Place the 5 back-of-hand sts next to index finger onto a needle, then place the 7 palm sts next to index finger onto another needle. With RS facing, join MC to beg of needle holding 5 sts.

Set-up rnd: K5, pick up and knit 7 sts from base of the 5 sts CO for index finger; with another needle, k7, then use the backward-loop method to CO 5 sts—24 sts for middle finger; 26 sts rem on holder.

Arrange sts as evenly as possible on 3 dpn and join for working in rnds.

Next rnd: K5, dec 2 of the next 7 picked-up sts by working them as sl 1, k1, psso, k3, k2tog, then knit to end of rnd—22 sts rem.

Work even in St st until finger measures about 2¾" (7 cm) from pick-up rnd or reaches the middle of the wearer's fingernail.

Next rnd: *K1, k2tog, rep from * to last sts, k1—15 sts rem.

Next rnd: Knit.

Next rnd: *K2tog; rep from * to last st, k1—8 sts rem.

Cut yarn, leaving an 8" (20.5 cm) tail. Thread tail on a tapestry needle, draw through rem sts, pull tight to close hole, and fasten off on WS.

RING FINGER

Place the 5 back-of-hand sts next to middle finger onto a needle, then place the 7 palm sts next to middle finger onto another needle. With RS facing, join MC to beg of needle holding 5 sts.

Set-up rnd: K5, pick up and knit 7 sts from base of 5 sts CO for middle finger; with another needle, k7, then use the backward-loop method to CO 5 sts—24 sts for ring finger; 14 sts rem on holder.

Arrange sts as evenly as possible on 3 dpn and join for working in rnds.

Next rnd: K5, dec 2 of the next 7 picked-up sts by working them as sl 1, k1, psso, k3, k2tog, then knit to end of rnd—22 sts rem.

Work even in St st until finger measures about 2½" (6.5 cm) from pick-up rnd or reaches the middle of the wearer's fingernail.

Work fingertip as for middle finger.

LITTLE FINGER

Place rem 7 back-of-hand sts onto a needle, then place rem 7 palm sts onto another needle.

With RS facing, join MC to beg of needle holding back-of-hand sts.

Set-up rnd: K7, pick up and knit 7 sts from base of the 5 sts CO for ring finger; with another needle, k7—21 sts total.

Arrange sts evenly on 3 dpn and join for working in rnds.

Next rnd: K7, dec 2 of the next 7 picked-up sts by working them as sl 1, k1, psso, k3, k2tog, then knit to end of rnd—19 sts rem.

Work even in St st until finger measures about 1¾" (4.5 cm) from pick-up rnd or reaches the middle of the wearer's fingernail.

Next rnd: *K1, k2tog; rep from * to last st, k1—13 sts rem.

Next rnd: Knit.

Next rnd: *K2tog; rep from * to last st, k1—7 sts rem.

Cut yarn, leaving an 8" (20.5 cm) tail. Thread tail on a tapestry needle, draw through rem sts, pull tight to close hole, and fasten off on WS.

THUMB

Place 12 held thumb sts onto a dpn. With RS facing, join MC to beg of needle holding these sts.

Set-up rnd: Knit the 12 thumb sts, then with an empty needle, pick up and knit 1 st from the side of the thumb opening, pick up and knit 12 sts from the base of the sts CO above the thumb gap, and pick up and knit 1 st from the other side of the thumb opening—26 sts total.

Arrange sts so the 12 original held sts are on Needle 1, the next 7 sts are on Needle 2, and the last 7 sts are on Needle 3.

Next rnd: K12, sl 1, k1, psso, k10, k2tog—24 sts rem; 12 sts on Needle 1, 6 sts each on Needle 2 and Needle 3.

Work even in St st until thumb measures about 2¼" (5.5 cm) from pick-up rnd or reaches the middle of the wearer's thumbnail.

Next rnd: *K1, k2tog; rep from *—16 sts rem.

Next rnd: Knit.

Next rnd: *K2tog; rep from *—8 sts rem.

Cut yarn, leaving an 8" (20.5 cm) tail. Thread tail on a tapestry needle, draw through rem sts, pull tight to close hole, and fasten off on WS.

Left Hand

Rnds begin at little-finger side of the hand, at start of palm sts.

Next rnd: (thumb placement, Rnd 20 of chart) Keeping in patt, work all 28 palm sts on Needle 1 and Needle 2, then place last 12 sts of Needle 2 onto a length of smooth cotton waste yarn; work all 28 back-of-hand sts on Needles 3 and 4 to end of rnd.

Next rnd: (Rnd 21 of chart) Work in patt to thumb gap of previous rnd, use the backward-loop method to CO 12 sts in chart patt across the gap, work in patt to end—still 56 sts.

Work Rnds 22–34 of chart—piece measures about 1¾" (4.5 cm) from thumb opening.

Try on glove to be sure it reaches to the base of your index and middle fingers. If not, work additional rnds with MC until hand is desired length.

Finger Set-Up

Move the last st from Needle 4 onto the beg of Needle 1, then move the first st from Needle 3 onto the end of

Needle 2—15 sts each on Needle 1 and Needle 2, 13 sts each on Needle 3 and Needle 4. As for right hand, fingers and thumb are worked in St st with MC.

INDEX FINGER

Set-up rnd: On Needle 1, k15; on Needle 2, knit the first 6 sts, place the last 21 sts worked onto cotton waste-yarn holder, then knit the rem 9 sts of Needle 2; with an empty needle, knit the first 9 sts of Needle 3, use the backward-loop method to CO 5 sts, then place rem 4 sts of Needle 3 and all 13 sts of Needle 4 onto other end of same waste-yarn holder—23 sts rem for index finger; 38 sts on holder.

Complete as for right-hand index finger.

MIDDLE FINGER

Place the 5 back-of-hand sts next to index finger onto a needle, then place the 7 palm sts next to index finger onto another needle. With RS facing, join MC to beg of needle holding 5 sts.

Set-up rnd: K5, use the backward-loop method to CO 5 sts; with another needle, k7, then pick up and knit 7 sts from base of the 5 sts CO for index finger—24 sts for middle finger; 26 sts rem on holder.

Complete as for right-hand middle finger.

RING FINGER

Place the 5 back-of-hand sts next to middle finger onto a needle, then place the 7 palm sts next to middle finger onto another needle. With RS facing, join MC to beg of needle holding 5 sts.

Set-up rnd: K5, use the backward-loop method to CO 5 sts; with another needle, k7, pick up and knit 7 sts from base of 5 sts CO for middle finger—24 sts for ring finger; 14 sts rem on holder.

Complete as for right-hand ring finger.

LITTLE FINGER

Place rem 7 back-of-hand sts onto a needle, then place rem 7 palm sts onto another needle.

With RS facing, join MC to beg of needle holding palm sts.

Set-up rnd: K7, pick up and knit 7 sts from base of the 5 sts CO for ring finger; with another needle, k7—21 sts total.

Complete as for right-hand little finger.

THUMB

Work as for right-hand thumb.

Finishing

Weave in all loose ends, using yarn tails to close up any holes between fingers as necessary.

Block to measurements.

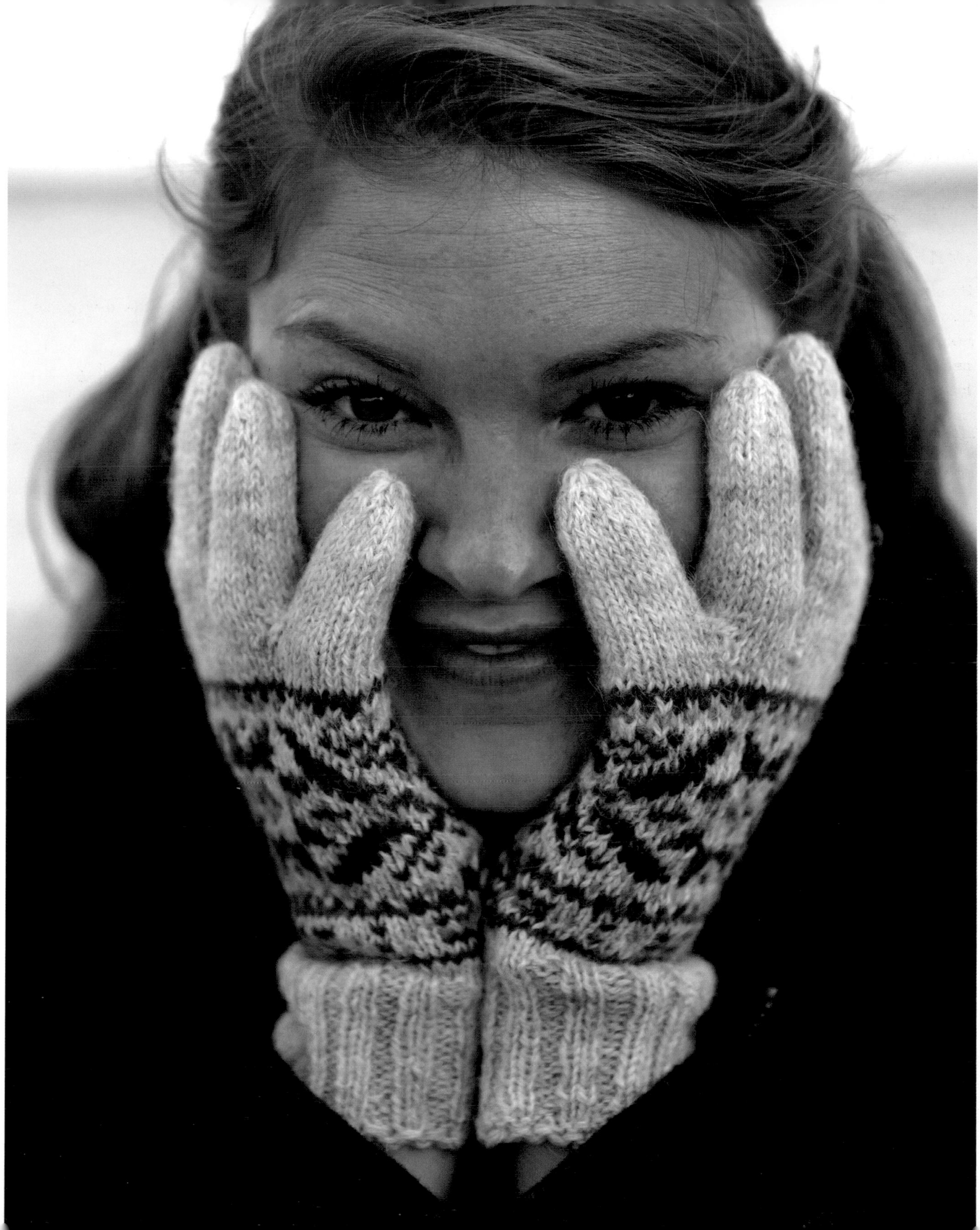

Morroless Socks

DESIGNED BY
MARY JANE
MUCKLESTONE

These socks reflect historical use of color in Fair Isle knitting. In addition to the natural colors of Shetland sheep, imported natural dyestuffs were originally used for blue and red, and local plants were used for yellow. With the advent of aniline dyes in the late nineteenth century, a host of new colors became available and were used in bold and sometimes garish combinations. Marking the intersection of the old with the new, I combined soft sheep's gray and lichen yellow patterned with a brilliant Norwegian star. I couldn't decide which color to use for the heel; hence the name *morroless*, which means "unmatched" or "odd" in Shetland dialect.

FINISHED SIZE

About 8" (20.5 cm) foot circumference, 9" (23 cm) leg length from CO to base of heel, and 9" (23 cm) foot length (adjustable).

YARN

Fingering weight (#1 Super Fine).

Shown Here: Jamieson & Smith 2-ply Jumper Weight (100% Shetland wool; 125 yd [114 m]/25 g): #203 grey (MC), #18 royal blue (A), #142 medium blue (B), #78 fawn heather (C), #121 yellow heather (D), #202 natural heather (E), #125 orange (F), and #79 kelly green (G), 1 ball each.

NEEDLES

Ribbing and stockinette sections: size U.S. 2 (2.75 mm): set of 5 double-pointed (dpn).

Charted section: size U.S. 3 (3.25 mm): set of 5 dpn.

Adjust needle size if necessary to obtain the correct gauge.

NOTIONS

Marker (m); tapestry needle.

GAUGE

14 sts and 20 rnds = 2" (5 cm) in single-color St st worked in rnds on smaller needles.

14 sts and 15 rnds = 2" (5 cm) in charted pattern worked in rnds on larger needles.

note

○ Stranded colorwork can produce a tighter gauge than single-color stockinette stitch, therefore the charted section of each sock is worked with larger needles than used for the ribbing or solid-color stockinette.

Leg

With MC and smaller needles, CO 64 sts. Divide sts evenly onto 4 needles (16 sts on each needle), place marker (pm), and join for working in rnds, being careful not to twist sts; rnd begins at center back leg.

Rib rnd: *K1, p1; rep from *.

Rep the rib rnd until piece measures about ¾" (2 cm) from CO.

With D, knit 1 rnd, then work 1 rib rnd.

With MC, knit 1 rnd, then work 2 rib rnds.

With D, knit 1 rnd, then work 1 rib rnd.

With MC, knit 1 rnd, then work 5 rib rnds—piece measures about 2" (5 cm) from CO.

Change to larger needles.

Next rnd: Work Rnd 1 of Morroless chart, working 16-st patt rep 4 times around.

Work Rnds 2–21 of chart—piece measures about 4¾" (12 cm) from CO.

Change to smaller needles.

With MC, work even in single-color St st until piece measures 1" (2.5 cm) from last rnd of chart—piece measures about 5¾" (14.5 cm) from CO.

Next rnd: K7, [k2tog, k14] 3 times, k2tog, k7—60 sts rem.

Work even in St st for 1" (2.5 cm) more—piece measures about 6¾" (17 cm) from CO.

Next rnd: K7, [k2tog, k13] 3 times, k2tog, k6—56 sts rem.

Work even in St st until piece measures 7" (18 cm) from CO.

Morroless

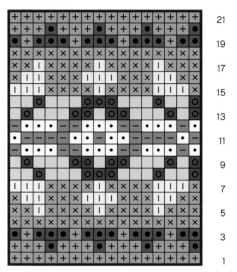

16-st repeat
work 4 times

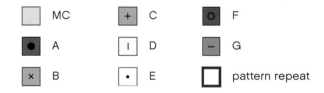

▢ MC	⊞ C	⊙ F
● A	▯ D	▬ G
⊠ B	⊡ E	▢ pattern repeat

Heel

Knit the first 14 sts, turn work.

Cut MC and join D for first sock heel (join B for second sock heel).

With WS facing, purl the 14 sts just worked onto a single dpn, then purl the next 14 sts onto the same dpn—28 heel sts total on one needle. Rem 28 sts will be worked later for instep.

Heel Flap

Work 28 heel sts back and forth in rows as foll:

Row 1: (RS) *Sl 1 as if to purl with yarn in back (pwise wyb), k1; rep from *.

Row 2: (WS) Sl 1 pwise with yarn in front (wyf), p27.

Rep the last 2 rows 13 more times—14 chain sts along each selvedge; heel flap measures about 2" (5 cm) high.

Heel Turn

Work short-rows as foll:

Row 1: (RS) Sl 1 pwise wyb, k15, ssk, k1, turn work.

Row 2: Sl 1 pwise wyf, p5, p2tog, p1, turn work.

Row 3: Sl 1 pwise wyb, knit to 1 st before gap formed on previous RS row, ssk (1 st from each side of gap), k1, turn work.

Row 4: Sl 1 pwise wyf, purl to 1 st before gap formed on previous WS row, p2tog (1 st from each side of gap), p1, turn work.

Rep Rows 3 and 4 four more times, omitting the final k1 on the last rep of Row 3 and the final p1 on the last rep of Row 4—16 sts rem.

Shape Gussets

Cut heel color and rejoin MC to beg of heel sts with RS facing.

Rejoin for working in rnds as foll:

Set-up rnd: With Needle 1, k16 heel sts, then pick up and knit 1 st in each of the 14 chain sts along edge of heel flap; with Needle 2, k28 instep sts; with Needle 3, pick up and knit 1 st in each of the 14 chain sts along edge of heel flap, then knit the first 8 heel sts again—72 sts total; 22 sts on Needle 1; 28 sts on Needle 2; 22 sts on Needle 3.

Rnd begs at center of heel, in middle of sole of foot.

Rnd 1: On Needle 1, knit to last 3 sts, k2tog, k1; on Needle 2, knit; on Needle 3, k1, ssk, knit to end—2 sts dec'd; 1 st dec'd each on Needle 1 and Needle 3.

Rnd 2: Knit.

Rep Rnds 1 and 2 seven more times—56 sts rem; 14 sts on Needle 1; 28 sts on Needle 2; 14 sts on Needle 3.

Foot

Work even in St st until foot measures 6" (15 cm) from center back heel, or about 3" (7.5 cm) less than desired total length.

With D, knit 2 rnds.

With MC, knit 3 rnds.

With D, knit 2 rnds.

With MC, knit 2 rnds—foot measures about 7" (18 cm) from center back heel, or 2" (5 cm) less than desired length.

Cut MC.

Shape Toe

Cont with D as foll:

Rnd 1: On Needle 1, knit to last 3 sts, k2tog, k1; on Needle 2, k1, ssk, work to last 3 sts, k2tog, k1; on Needle 3, k1, ssk, knit to end—4 sts dec'd.

Rnd 2: Knit.

Rep Rnds 1 and 2 six more times—28 sts rem.

Rep Rnd 1 (i.e., dec every rnd) four times—12 sts rem; 3 sts on Needle 1; 6 sts on Needle 2; 3 sts on Needle 3.

Knit the 3 sts from Needle 1 onto the end of Needle 3— 6 sts each on 2 needles.

Finishing

Cut yarn, leaving a 12" (30.5 cm) tail. Thread tail on tapestry needle and use the Kitchener st (see Glossary) to graft rem sts tog.

Weave in loose ends. Block lightly.

Mirry-Dancers Yoked Pullover

DESIGNED BY CHERYL BURKE

For the colorwork pattern in this yoked pullover, **Cheryl Burke** drew upon her fascination with the natural light displays in high-latitude skies, called "aurora borealis" or "northern lights." Known as *mirry dancers* in Shetland dialect, these light displays are famously spectacular in the Shetland Islands. Like the colors in the sky, Cheryl's unexpected color combinations form a large-scale design in a small rhythmic pattern. Placed around the yoke of a dark seamless pullover, with accents at the cuffs and hem, the effect is luminous bursts of color shooting through the dark.

FINISHED SIZE

About 33 (35, 39, 44, 49, 53)" (84 [89, 99, 112, 124.5, 134.5] cm) bust circumference.

Sweater shown measures 35" (89 cm).

YARN

Sportweight (#2 Fine).

Shown here: Jamieson's Double Knitting (100% pure Shetland wool; 82 yd [75 m]/25 g): #293 port wine (MC), 10 (11, 14, 16, 18, 20) skeins; #710 gentian (CC1; navy), #435 apricot (CC2), #308 tangerine (CC3), #1020 nighthawk (CC4; dark teal), #688 mermaid (CC5; peacock), #470 pumpkin (CC6), and #462 ginger (CC7; rust), 1 (1, 1, 1, 1, 1) skein each; #812 prairie (CC8; dark green), 1 (1, 1, 2, 2, 3) skein(s); #587 madder (CC9; brown), 2 (2, 2, 3, 3, 4) skeins; #259 leprechaun (CC10; light green), 1 (1, 2, 2, 2, 3) skein(s).

NEEDLES

Size U.S. 5 (3.75 mm): 16" and 24" (40 and 60 cm) circular (cir) and set of 5 double-pointed (dpn).

Adjust needle size if necessary to obtain the correct gauge.

NOTIONS

Markers (m); stitch holders; tapestry needle.

GAUGE

24 sts and 32 rnds = 4" (10 cm) in St st and charted patt, worked in rnds.

stitch guide

Corrugated Rib (multiple of 4 sts)

Rnds 1–4: *K2 with CC1, p2 with MC; rep from *.

Rnds 5–8: *K2 with CC4, p2 with MC; rep from *.

Rnds 9 and 10: *K2 with CC5, p2 with MC; rep from *.

Rnds 11 and 12: *K2 with CC5, p2 with CC9; rep from *.

Rnds 13–16: *K2 with CC8, p2 with CC9; rep from *.

Rnds 17–20: *K2 with CC10, p2 with CC9; rep from *.

notes

○ This sweater is worked in the round from the top down.

○ When working the yoke, change to longer circular needle when necessary.

○ The corrugated rib is a k2, p2 rib in which the knit stitches are worked in one color and the purl stitches are worked in a second color as follows: *With both colors in back, k2 with the knit color, bring the purl color to the front and p2, then bring the purl color to the back again; repeat from * for the pattern. The unused color should always be stranded across the WS of the work.

● MC		○ CC6		− CC10	
I CC3		+ CC7		M M1 with color shown	
▲ CC4		◇ CC8		no stitch	
× CC5		II CC9		pattern repeat	

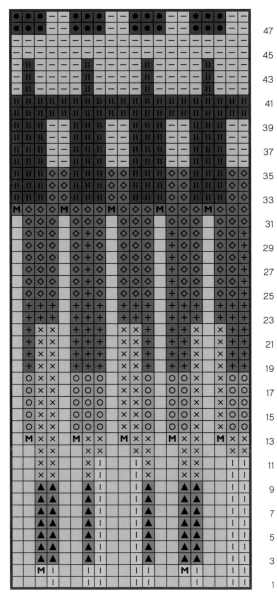

Yoke Chart A

8-st repeat
inc'd to 20-st repeat

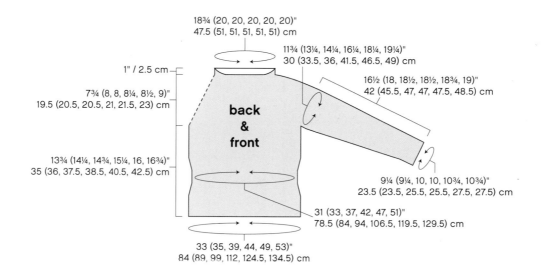

18¾ (20, 20, 20, 20, 20)"
47.5 (51, 51, 51, 51, 51) cm

11¾ (13¼, 14¼, 16¼, 18¼, 19¼)"
30 (33.5, 36, 41.5, 46.5, 49) cm

1" / 2.5 cm

16½ (18, 18½, 18½, 18¾, 19)"
42 (45.5, 47, 47, 47.5, 48.5) cm

7¾ (8, 8, 8¼, 8½, 9)"
19.5 (20.5, 20.5, 21, 21.5, 23) cm

back & front

13¾ (14¼, 14¾, 15¼, 16, 16¾)"
35 (36, 37.5, 38.5, 40.5, 42.5) cm

9¼ (9¼, 10, 10, 10¾, 10¾)"
23.5 (23.5, 25.5, 25.5, 27.5, 27.5) cm

31 (33, 37, 42, 47, 51)"
78.5 (84, 94, 106.5, 119.5, 129.5) cm

33 (35, 39, 44, 49, 53)"
84 (89, 99, 112, 124.5, 134.5) cm

Yoke

With CC1 and 16" (40 cm) cir needle, CO 112 (120, 120, 120, 120, 120) sts. Place marker (pm) and join for working in rnds, being careful not to twist sts; rnd begins at right side of neck.

Neckband

Set-up rnd: With CC1, *k2, p2; rep from *.

Join CC2.

Rnds 1–6: Work corrugated rib (see Notes) as foll: *K2 with CC2, p2 with CC1; rep from *—piece measures 1" (2.5 cm) after completing Rnd 6.

Change to CC3. Work 48 (48, 48, 53, 53, 55) rnds of Yoke Chart A (A, A, B, B, C; see pages 30 and 31 for charts B and C), changing colors and inc as shown—280 (300, 300, 375, 375, 450) sts.

Next rnd: With MC, k140 (150, 150, 188, 188, 225), pm for left side, knit to end—yoke measures 6 (6, 6, 6¾, 6¾, 7)" (15,

[15, 15, 17, 17, 18] cm) from last neckband rnd and about 1" (2.5) cm longer from CO.

Raise Back Neck

Work short-rows (see Glossary) as foll:

Short-Row 1: (RS) K10, wrap next st, turn work.

Short-Row 2: P10, sl end-of-rnd m, purl to left side m, sl m, p10, turn work.

Short-Row 3: K10, sl left side m, knit to 12 sts before previously wrapped st, wrap next st, turn work.

Short-Row 4: Purl to 12 sts before previously wrapped st, wrap next st, turn work.

Short-Rows 5–8: Rep Short-Rows 3 and 4 two more times.

Knit to end-of-rnd m, then knit 1 complete rnd, working the wraps tog with the wrapped sts and removing left side m as you come to it—yoke measures about 7¼ (7¼, 7¼, 8, 8, 8¼)" (18.5 [18.5, 18.5, 20.5, 20.5, 21] cm) from last neckband rnd at center back and about 1" (2.5) cm less at center front.

Yoke Chart B

8-st repeat
inc'd to 25-st repeat

Cont for your size as foll:

SIZE 39" ONLY

Next rnd: *K10, M1 (see Glossary); rep from*—330 sts.

SIZE 49" ONLY

Next rnd: *[K8, M1 (see Glossary)] 2 times, k9, M1; rep from *—420 sts.

ALL SIZES

Knit 4 (6, 5, 2, 3, 6) rnds, dec 0 (0, 0, 1, 0, 0) st in last rnd—280 (300, 330, 374, 420, 450) sts; yoke measures 7¾ (8, 8, 8¼, 8½, 9)" (19.5 [20.5, 20.5, 21, 21.5, 23] cm) from end of neckband at center back and 1" (2.5 cm) less at center front.

Separate Body and Sleeves

Dividing rnd: With MC, k28 (31, 34, 38, 43, 46) for front half of right sleeve and place sts on holder, k84 (88, 98, 111, 124, 134) front sts, place next 56 (62, 67, 76, 86, 91) sts on holder for left sleeve, use the backward-loop method (see Glossary) to CO 7 (8, 9, 10, 11, 12) sts, pm for left side, CO 8 (9, 10, 11, 12, 13) more sts, k84 (88, 98, 111, 124, 134) back sts, place rem 28 (31, 33, 38, 43, 45) sts for back half of right sleeve on holder with other right sleeve sts, CO 7 (8, 9, 10, 11, 12) sts, pm for right side and end-of-rnd, CO 8 (9, 10, 11, 12, 13) more sts—198 (210, 234, 264, 294, 318) sts rem.

● MC		○ CC6		— CC10	
I CC3		+ CC7		M M1 with color shown	
▲ CC4		◇ CC8		no stitch	
× CC5		‖ CC9		☐ pattern repeat	

Yoke Chart C

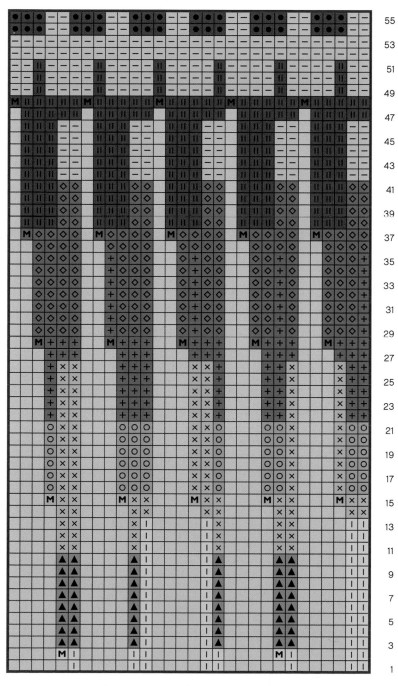

8-st repeat inc'd to 30-st repeat

Body

With MC, knit to end-of-rnd m. Work even in St st with MC until piece measures 4½ (5, 5, 5½, 5¾, 6)" (11.5 [12.5, 12.5, 14, 14.5, 15] cm) from dividing rnd.

Shape Waist

Dec rnd: K1, ssk, knit to 3 sts before side m, k2tog, k1, sl m, k1, ssk, knit to last 3 sts, k2tog, k1—4 sts dec'd.

[Work 6 (6, 6, 6, 7, 7) rnds even, then rep the dec rnd] 2 times—186 (198, 222, 252, 282, 306) sts rem.

Work even in St st for 14 (16, 16, 18, 18, 20) rnds—piece measures 8¼ (9, 9, 9¾, 10¼, 10¾)" (21 [23, 23, 25, 26, 27.5] cm) from dividing rnd.

Inc rnd: K1, M1L (see Glossary), knit to 1 st before side m, M1R (see Glossary), k1, sl m, k1, M1L, knit to last st, M1R, k1— 4 sts inc'd.

[Work 6 (6, 6, 6, 7, 7) rnds even, then rep the inc rnd] 2 times—198 (210, 234, 264, 294, 318) sts. Work in St st until piece measures 10¾ (11¼, 11¾, 12¼, 13, 13¾)" (27.5 [28.5, 30, 31, 33, 35] cm) from dividing rnd, and *at the same time* inc 2 (2, 2, 0, 2, 2) sts evenly spaced in last rnd—200 (212, 236, 264, 296, 320) sts.

Lower Edge Rib

Join CC1 and work Rnds 1–20 of corrugated rib patt (see Stitch Guide and Notes).

Next rnd: With CC9, *k2, p2; rep from *—piece measures 13¾ (14¼, 14¾, 15¼, 16, 16¾)" (35 [36, 37.5, 38.5, 40.5, 42.5] cm) from dividing rnd.

Loosely BO all sts in rib patt with CC9.

Sleeves

Place 56 (62, 67, 76, 86, 91) held sleeve sts on 4 dpn, distributed as evenly as possible. Join MC in center of underarm CO sts. Pick up and knit 8 (9, 10, 11, 12, 13) sts along half of underarm CO sts, knit to end of sleeve sts, pick up and knit 7 (8, 9, 10, 11, 12) sts along other half of CO sts, pm for end of rnd—71 (79, 86, 97, 109, 116) sts total.

Work even in St st until piece measures 1¾ (2, 2¼, 2½, 3, 3)" (4.5 [5, 5.5, 6.5, 7.5, 7.5] cm) from dividing rnd.

Dec rnd: K1, k2tog, knit to last 3 sts, ssk, k1—2 sts dec'd.

[Work 13 (8, 7, 4, 3, 3) rnds even, then rep the dec rnd] 6 (10, 12, 17, 21, 25) times—57 (57, 60, 61, 65, 64) sts rem. Knit 1 rnd, and *at the same time* dec 1 (1, 0, 1, 1, 0) st—56 (56, 60, 60, 64, 64) sts. Work even in St st until sleeve measures 13½ (15, 15½, 15½, 15¾, 16)" (34.5 [38, 39.5, 39.5, 40, 40.5] cm) from dividing rnd or 3" (7.5 cm) less than desired total length.

Join CC1 and work Rnds 1–20 of corrugated rib patt as for lower body.

Next rnd: With CC9, *k2, p2; rep from *—piece measures 16½ (18, 18½, 18½, 18¾, 19)" (42 [45.5, 47, 47, 47.5, 48.5] cm) from dividing rnd.

With CC9, loosely BO all sts in rib patt.

Finishing

Weave in loose ends. Block to measurements.

Ketlin Skirt

DESIGNED BY KAT COYLE

Known for her vibrant use of color, **Kat Coyle** brilliantly marries a somber tone with dazzling brights in this short skirt that includes two of her son's favorite things—black cats and the color red. Though the cat motif is an old one, the skirt is both youthful and classic— wear it with boots in deep winter or with sandals in high summer. A drawstring allows it to be cinched in at the waist or ride low on the hips. For fun, Kat made an alternate drawstring with stripes in the colors of the Fair Isle patterning; it doubles as a cool bracelet!

FINISHED SIZE

About 26¾ (29¼, 32, 34¾, 37¼, 40)" (68 [74.5, 81.5, 88.5, 94.5, 101.5] cm) waist circumference without drawstring, 33½ (36¼, 38¾, 41½, 44¼, 46¾)" (85 [92, 98.5, 105.5, 112.5, 118.5] cm) hip circumference, 40¾ (43¼, 45¾, 48¼, 51, 53½)" (103.5 [110, 116, 122.5, 129.5, 136] lower edge circumference, and 17½ (17½, 19½, 19½, 20½, 20½)" (44.5 [44.5, 49.5, 49.5, 52, 52] cm) long.

Skirt shown measures 36¼" (92 cm) at hip.

YARN

Sportweight (#2 Fine).

Shown here: St-Denis Nordique (100% wool; 150 yd [137 m]/50 g): #5875 elephant (MC; taupe), 3 (3, 4, 5, 5, 6) skeins; #5858 red (CC1), #5813 black (CC2), #5836 oatmeal (CC3), #5803 grey card (CC4), #5820 blue eggshell (CC5), #5850 soft yellow (CC6), #5825 spicy rose (CC7), #5816 champagne (CC8), 1 skein each.

NEEDLES

Body: size U.S. 6 (4 mm): 24" circular (cir).

Waistband and drawstring: size U.S. 4 (3.5 mm): 24" (60 cm) circular and set of 2 double-pointed (dpn).

Adjust needle size if necessary to obtain the correct gauge.

NOTIONS

Markers (m); tapestry needle.

GAUGE

21 sts and 30 rnds = 4" (10 cm) in solid-color St st on larger needle worked in rnds, after blocking.

22 sts and 26 rnds = 4" (10 cm) in Ketlin chart patt on larger needle worked in rnds, after blocking.

note

○ This skirt is worked in rounds from the hem to the waistband and is designed to have 2" (5 cm) negative ease at the hips.

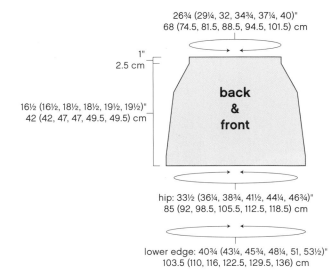

26¾ (29¼, 32, 34¾, 37¼, 40)"
68 (74.5, 81.5, 88.5, 94.5, 101.5) cm

1"
2.5 cm

back & front

16½ (16½, 18½, 18½, 19½, 19½)"
42 (42, 47, 47, 49.5, 49.5) cm

hip: 33½ (36¼, 38¾, 41½, 44¼, 46¾)"
85 (92, 98.5, 105.5, 112.5, 118.5) cm

lower edge: 40¾ (43¼, 45¾, 48¼, 51, 53½)"
103.5 (110, 116, 122.5, 129.5, 136) cm

Skirt

With CC1 and larger cir needle, CO 224 (238, 252, 266, 280, 294) sts. Place marker (pm) and join for working in rnds, being careful not to twist sts. Rnd begs at side "seam." Cut CC1.

Border

Rnd 1: With MC, *k1, p1; rep from *, placing another marker after 112 (119, 126, 133, 140, 147) sts to denote other side "seam."

Slip markers (sl m) every rnd as you come to them.

Rnds 2–4: Join CC3. *With both yarns in back, k1 MC, bring CC3 to front, p1 CC3, then bring CC3 to back; rep from *.

Rnd 5: Cut CC3. With MC, *k1, p1; rep from *—piece measures about 1" (2.5 cm) from CO.

Ketlin

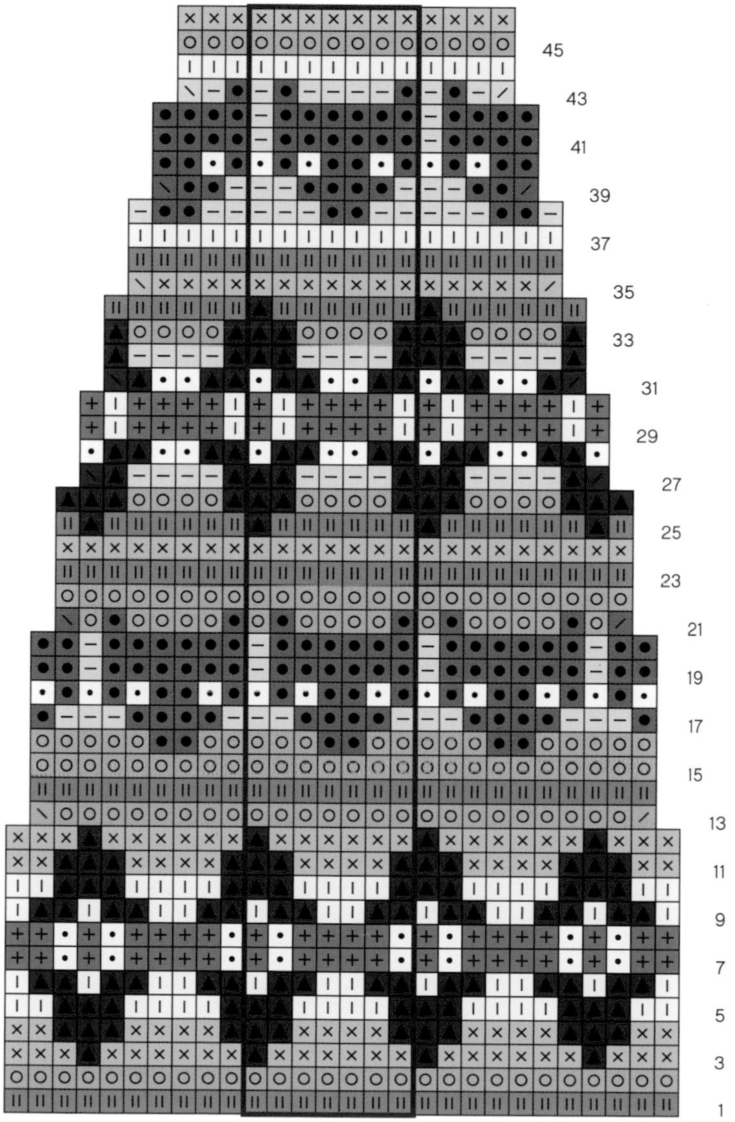

7-st repeat

| | | MC

■ CC1

● CC2

− CC3

○ CC4

× CC5

I CC6

+ CC7

• CC8

/ k2tog with color shown

\ ssk with color shown

☐ pattern repeat

Body

Next rnd: Set up patt from Rnd 1 of Ketlin chart (see page 37) as foll: *Work 11 sts before patt rep box once, work 7-st patt rep 13 (14, 15, 16, 17, 18) times, work 10 sts after patt rep box once, sl m; rep from * once more.

Cont in patt until Rnd 12 of chart has been completed.

Next rnd: (dec rnd, Rnd 13 of chart) *K2tog with color shown, work to patt rep box, work 7-st patt rep 13 (14, 15, 16, 17, 18) times, work to 2 sts before side m, ssk; rep from * once more—4 sts dec'd.

Cont in patt, Work Rnds 14–46 of chart, dec 4 sts in the same manner as Rnd 13 in Rnds 21, 27, 31, 35, 39, and 43—196 (210, 224, 238, 252, 266) sts rem; 98 (105, 112, 119, 126, 133) sts each for front and back.

Next rnd: With MC, knit and *at the same time* dec 20 sts evenly spaced—176 (190, 204, 218, 232, 246) sts rem; 88 (95, 102, 109, 116, 123) sts each for front and back.

Work even in St st until piece measures 12 (12, 14, 14, 15, 15)" (30.5 [30.5, 35.5, 35.5, 38, 38] cm) from CO.

Dec rnd: *K2tog, knit to 2 sts before side m, ssk, sl m; rep from * once—4 sts dec'd.

[Knit 3 rnds even, then rep the dec rnd] 8 times—140 (154, 168, 182, 196, 210) sts rem; 70 (77, 84, 91, 98, 105) sts each for front and back.

Work even if necessary until piece measures 16½ (16½, 18½, 18½, 19½, 19½)" (42 [42, 47, 47, 49.5, 49.5] cm) from CO.

Waistband

Change to smaller cir needle.

Rnds 1–3: *K1 through back loop (tbl), p1; rep from *.

Rnd 4: (drawstring eyelet rnd) *K2tog tbl, yo, k1tbl, p1; rep from * to last 0 (2, 0, 2, 0, 2) sts, work [k2tog tbl, yo] 0 (1, 0, 1, 0, 1) time.

Rnds 5–7: *K1tbl, p1; rep from *.

BO all sts.

Finishing

Block to measurements. Weave in loose ends.

Drawstring

With MC and smaller dpn, CO 3 sts. Work 3-st I-cord (see Glossary) until piece measures 43 (45, 48, 50, 53, 55)" (109 [114.5, 122, 127, 134.5, 139.5] cm) from CO.

Next rnd: K3tog—1 st rem.

Cut yarn and pull loop until tail comes free. Weave in loose ends.

Beginning and ending at center front, thread drawstring through eyelets in Rnd 4 of waistband and tie in a bow as shown.

Optional Striped Drawstring/Bracelet

Using leftovers of all colors, work as for solid-color drawstring in 1" (2.5 cm) stripes.

Mushroom Kelliemuffs

DESIGNED BY
SPILLYJANE,
A.K.A. JANE DUPUIS

Called *kelliemuffs* in old Shetland dialect, fingerless mittens are ideal for excursions on cool, but not quite cold, fall days. For the mitts shown here, **SpillyJane** (also known as **Jane Dupuis**) incorporated an appealing mushroom motif between small peerie bands, all in lovely autumn colors. The simple construction in these small mitts makes them a nice introduction to stranded knitting. There's no thumb gusset to interrupt the pattern, and the small motifs are repeated throughout. You'll be out hunting mushrooms in style and comfort in no time!

FINISHED SIZE

About 7" (18 cm) hand circumference and 7½" (19 cm) long.

YARN

Fingering weight (#1 Super Fine).

Shown here: Sunday Knits Nirvana 3-ply (92% merino, 8% cashmere; 246 yd [225 m]/50 g): earth (MC; dark brown) and sand (CC2), 1 skein each.

Sunday Knits Angelic 3-ply (75% merino, 25% angora; 246 yd [225 m]/50 g): wren (CC1; medium brown), 1 skein.

Sunday Knits Brigadoon 3-ply (100% merino; 246 yd [225 m]/50 g): birch (CC3; light gray), 1 skein.

Sunday Knits Eden 3-ply (100% merino; 246 yd [225 m]/50 g): red (CC4), 1 skein.

NEEDLES

Size U.S. 2 (2.75 mm): set of 5 double-pointed (dpn).

Adjust needle size if necessary to obtain the correct gauge.

NOTIONS

Marker (m); smooth fingering-weight waste yarn in contrasting color; tapestry needle.

GAUGE

32 sts and 30½ rnds = 4" (10 cm) in charted patt, worked in rnds.

Mitt

With CC3 and using the long-tail method (see Glossary), CO 56 sts.

Arrange sts evenly on 4 dpn (14 sts on each needle), place marker (pm), and join for working in rnds, being careful not to twist sts.

Cuff

Rib rnd: *[K1 through back loop (tbl)] 2 times, p2; rep from *.

Rep this rnd 9 more times—10 rnds total; piece measures about 1" (2.5 cm) from CO.

Hand

Next rnd: Work Rnd 1 of Kelliemuffs chart, working the 14-st patt rep 4 times around.

Cont in chart patt as established, work Rnds 2–28 of chart—piece measures about 4½" (11.5 cm) from CO.

Next rnd: (thumb placement, Rnd 29 of chart) K2 with MC, use contrasting waste yarn to knit the next 10 sts, return the 10 sts just worked to left needle, then knit to end of rnd with MC—the 10 thumb sts will have been worked twice, once with waste yarn and once with MC.

Work Rnds 30–46 of chart—piece measures about 7" (18 cm) from CO.

Top Ribbing

Rib rnd: [K1tbl] 2 times, p2; rep from *.

Rep this rnd 4 more times—5 rnds total; piece measures about 7½" (19 cm) from CO.

Loosely BO all sts in rib patt.

Thumb

Carefully remove waste yarn from thumb sts and place 10 exposed sts from top and bottom of thumb opening on separate dpn. With RS facing, join CC3 to beg of sts on one needle.

Rnd 1: *Pick up and knit 1 st in corner before thumb sts, k10, pick up and knit 1 st in corner after thumb sts; rep from * for other needle—24 sts total.

Arrange sts evenly on 3 needles (8 sts on each needle).

Rnds 2 and 3: With CC3, knit.

Rnds 4–9: *[K1tbl] 2 times, p2; rep from *—thumb measures about 1" (2.5 cm) after Rnd 9.

Loosely BO all sts in rib patt.

Finishing

Weave in loose ends. Place mitts under a damp tea towel and press with a hot iron to steam-block.

Kelliemuffs

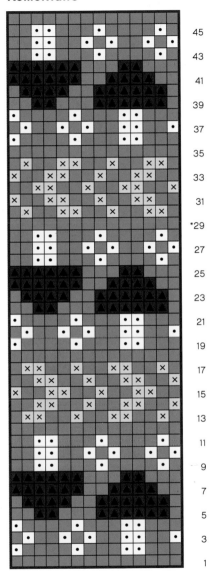

14-st repeat

*Thumb placment rnd;
see instructions.

 MC

 CC1

 CC2

 CC4

pattern repeat

Mirknin Hat and Scarf

DESIGNED BY
ELINOR BROWN

A perfect introduction to traditional Fair Isle knitting, the classic OXO pattern arrangement, with its easy-to-read-and-memorize geometric motif, makes **Elinor Brown's** hat and scarf accessible to knitters new to stranded colorwork. The background is worked in shades of blue accented by brilliant and unexpected colors for the pattern group— green, orange, yellow, and red. The stitch pattern is repeated along the length of the tubular scarf. The hat showcases three bands of the same OXO motif, the first of which is worked simultaneously with crown decreases unobtrusively and elegantly centered in each O.

FINISHED SIZE

Hat: About 21¼" (54 cm) head circumference.

Scarf: About 5¼" (13.5 cm) wide and 54½" (138.5 cm) long.

YARN

Sportweight (#2 Fine).

Shown here: Jamieson's Double Knitting (100% pure Shetland wool; 82 yd [75 m]/25 g): #150 Atlantic (MC; navy heather), 8 skeins; #168 Clyde blue (CC1; dark blue), #136 Teviot (CC2; medium blue), #1140 Granny Smith (CC3; lime green),

#1160 Scotch broom (CC4; gold), and #478 amber (CC5; orange), 3 skeins each; #134 blue Danube (CC6; light blue), and #587 madder (CC7; red-brown), 2 skeins each.

Note: Yarn amounts are for the set, including both hat and scarf.

NEEDLES

Size U.S. 5 (3.75 mm): 16" (40 cm) circular (cir) and set of 4 or 5 double-pointed (dpn).

Adjust needle size if necessary to obtain the correct gauge.

NOTIONS

Spare needle in same size as main needles; waste yarn; markers (m); tapestry needle.

GAUGE

25 sts and 27½ rnds = 4" (10 cm) in charted patts, worked in rnds.

Hat

With MC and 1 dpn, CO 6 sts. Arrange sts as evenly as possible on 3 or 4 dpn. Place m (pm) and join for working in rnds, being careful not to twists sts.

Next rnd: *K1, M1 (see Glossary); rep from *—12 sts.

Knit 1 rnd even.

Work Rnds 1–26 of Hat chart, inc as shown and changing to 16" (40 cm) cir needle when necessary—132 sts. Work Rnds 27–42 of chart 2 times.

Next rnd: *K2, p2; rep from *.

Rep the last rnd once more. Loosely BO all sts in rib patt.

Scarf

With MC, waste yarn, and 16" (40 cm) cir needle, use a provisional method (see Glossary) to CO 33 sts.

Knit 1 row.

Carefully remove waste yarn from provisional CO and place 32 exposed sts from base of CO onto spare needle, k32, M1 (see Glossary), place marker (pm) and join for working in rnds—66 sts total; 33 sts on each needle.

Note: *Because the end of the scarf is closed, you will need to work across each needle separately for the first few rounds; change to dpn when the scarf is long enough to open into a tube.*

Work Rnds 1–16 of Scarf chart 23 times, then work Rnds 1–5 once more—374 rnds total including beg rnd; piece measures about 54½" (138.5 cm) from CO.

Cut yarn, leaving a 24" (61 cm) tail.

Flatten scarf and distribute sts evenly onto two needles so that there are 33 sts on each needle to correspond to the sts at the beg of the scarf. With yarn threaded on a tapestry needle, use the Kitchener st (see Glossary) to graft sts tog.

Finishing

Block pieces to measurements. Weave in loose ends.

Hat

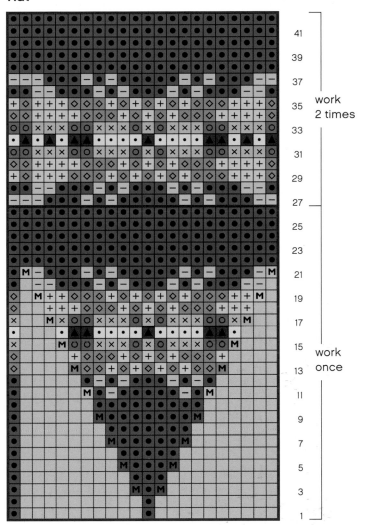

2-st repeat inc'd to 22-st repeat

Scarf

22-st repeat

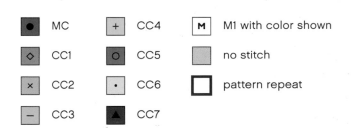

● MC	+ CC4	M M1 with color shown
◇ CC1	O CC5	no stitch
× CC2	• CC6	□ pattern repeat
− CC3	▲ CC7	

Bressay Dress

DESIGNED BY GUDRUN JOHNSTON

For this Fair Isle dress, **Gudrun Johnston** took inspiration from a knitted dress that her mother designed for her Shetland knitwear business in the 1970s. While her mother's design reached the floor and featured a turtleneck and oversized sleeves, Gudrun opted for a circular-yoke design in a more manageable length with cap sleeves and decorative semicircular pockets. The Fair Isle patterns are all simple repeats, and the top-down construction allows the garment to be tried on to get the best fit and length. Worked in subtle tweedy shades of Brooklyn Tweed Loft, this dress has a soft, swingy drape.

FINISHED SIZE

About 32½ (36¼, 39¾, 43¼, 46¼, 49¾)" (82.5 [92, 101, 110, 117.5, 126.5] cm) bust circumference.

Note: This dress is designed for a close fit at the yoke and up to 1" (2.5 cm) ease at the bust.

Dress shown measures 36¼" (92 cm).

YARN

Fingering weight (#1 Super Fine).

Shown here: Brooklyn Tweed Loft (100% Targhee-Columbia American wool; 275 yd [251 m]/ 50 g): #08 truffle hunt (MC; brown), 6 (6, 7, 7, 8, 8) skeins; #22 faded quilt (CC1; light blue), #21 hayloft (CC2; gold), #27 woodsmoke (CC3; beige), 1 skein each for all sizes.

NEEDLES

Size U.S. 4 (3.5 mm): 16", 24", 32", and 40" (40, 60, 80, and 100 cm) circular (cir) and set of 4 or 5 double-pointed (dpn).

Adjust needle size if necessary to obtain the correct gauge.

NOTIONS

Markers (m); waste yarn; tapestry needle.

GAUGE

27 sts and 36 rows/rnds = 4" (10 cm) in solid-color St st and charted patterns.

notes

○ This dress is worked seamlessly from the top down.

○ The colorwork charts (see page 53) are worked in rounds for the yoke and body; back and forth in rows for the pockets. When working charts in the round, read every chart row from right to left as a RS round. When working in rows for the pockets, read odd-numbered RS rows from right to left and read even-numbered WS rows from left to right.

Neckband

With MC and 16" (40 cm) cir needle, CO 120 (120, 128, 128, 136, 136) sts.

Place marker (pm) and join for working in rnds, being careful not to twist sts. Rnd begins at center back.

Rib rnd: *K2, p2; rep from *.

Rep the rib rnd 3 more times.

Knit 1 rnd.

Inc Rnd 1: *K4, M1 (see Glossary); rep from *—150 (150, 160, 160, 170, 170) sts.

Knit 1 rnd—piece measures about ¾" (2 cm) from CO.

Shape Back Neck

Work back and forth in short-rows (see Glossary) to add length to the back neck (centered over the end-of-rnd m) as foll:

Short-Row 1: (RS) K32 (32, 36, 36, 40, 40), wrap next st, turn work.

Short-Row 2: (WS) P64 (64, 72, 72, 80, 80), wrap next st, turn work.

Short-Row 3: Knit to wrapped st, work wrap tog with wrapped st, k5, wrap next st, turn work.

Short-Row 4: Purl to wrapped st, work wrap tog with wrapped st, p5, wrap next st, turn work.

Short-Rows 5 and 6: Rep Short-Rows 3 and 4.

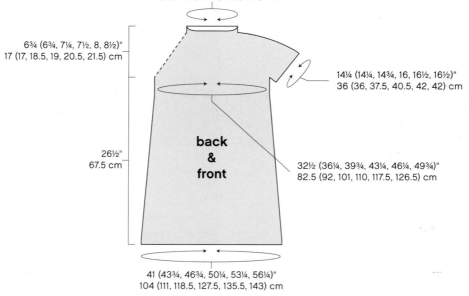

17¾ (17¾, 19, 19, 20¼, 20¼)"
45 (45, 48.5, 48.5, 51.5, 51.5) cm

6¾ (6¾, 7¼, 7½, 8, 8½)"
17 (17, 18.5, 19, 20.5, 21.5) cm

14¼ (14¼, 14¾, 16, 16½, 16½)"
36 (36, 37.5, 40.5, 42, 42) cm

back & front

26½"
67.5 cm

32½ (36¼, 39¾, 43¼, 46¼, 49¾)"
82.5 (92, 101, 110, 117.5, 126.5) cm

41 (43¾, 46¾, 50¼, 53¼, 56¼)"
104 (111, 118.5, 127.5, 135.5, 143) cm

Next row: (RS) Knit to end-of-rnd m.

Knit 1 rnd across all sts, working wraps tog with wrapped sts when you come to them.

Knit 1 rnd even—piece measures about 1½" (3.8 cm) from CO at center back and about ¾" (2 cm) less at center front.

Note: *All following yoke lengths are measured from center back neck.*

Inc Rnd 2: Change to 24" (60 cm) cir needle and work for your size as foll:

SIZE 32½" ONLY

*K7, M1, [k3, M1] 6 times; rep from *—192 sts.

SIZE 36¼" ONLY

*K3, M1; rep from *—200 sts.

SIZE 39¾" ONLY

*K5, M1, [k3, M1] 5 times; rep from *—208 sts.

SIZE 43¼" ONLY

*K2, M1, [k3, M1] 6 times; rep from *—216 sts.

SIZE 46¼" ONLY

K1, M1, *k3, M1; rep from * to last st, k1, M1—228 sts.

SIZE 49¾" ONLY

K3, M1, *[k2, M1] 7 times, [k3, M1] 9 times; rep from * to last 3 sts, k3, M1—236 sts.

ALL SIZES

Work Rnds 1–11 of Chart A (see page 53).

Inc Rnd 3: Working Rnd 12 of Chart A, work for your size as foll:

SIZE 32½" ONLY

*K6, M1, [k3, M1] 14 times; rep from *—252 sts.

SIZE 36¼" ONLY

*K4, M1, [k3, M1] 7 times; rep from *—264 sts.

SIZE 39¾" ONLY

*K4, M1, [k3, M1] 16 times; rep from *—276 sts.

SIZE 43¼" ONLY

*K3, M1; rep from *—288 sts.

SIZE 46¼" ONLY

*K4, M1, [k3, M1] 5 times; rep from *—300 sts.

SIZE 49¾" ONLY

*K5, M1, [k3, M1] 24 times; rep from * to last 5 sts, k5, M1—312 sts.

ALL SIZES

Change to 32" (80 cm) cir needle. Work Rnds 13–15 of Chart A, then Rnds 1–7 of Chart B, then work Rnds 1–4 of Chart A again—piece measures about 4½" (11.5 cm) from CO.

Inc Rnd 4: Working Rnd 5 of Chart A, work for your size as foll:

SIZE 32½" ONLY

*K7, M1, [k8, M1] 7 times; rep from *—284 sts.

SIZE 36¼" ONLY

*K10, M1, [k7, M1] 8 times; rep from *—300 sts.

Chart A

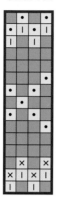

15
13
11
9
7
5
3
1

4-st
repeat

Chart B

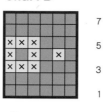

7
5
3
1

6-st repeat

Chart C

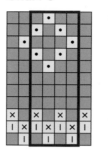

11
9
7
5
3
1

4-st
repeat

 MC

 CC1

 CC2

| · | CC3

| ▢ | pattern repeat

SIZE 39¾" ONLY

*K6, M1, [k7, M1] 9 times; rep from *—316 sts.

SIZE 43¼" ONLY

*K12, M1, [k6, M1] 10 times; rep from *—332 sts.

SIZE 46¼" ONLY

*K9, M1 [k6, M1] 11 times; rep from *—348 sts.

SIZE 49¾" ONLY

*K6, M1; rep from *—364 sts.

ALL SIZES

Work Rnds 6–15 of Chart A.

With MC, knit 1 rnd even.

Inc Rnd 5: Change to 40" (100 cm) cir needle. With MC, work for your size as foll:

SIZE 32½" ONLY

*K8, M1, [k7, M1] 9 times; rep from *—324 sts.

SIZE 36¼" ONLY

*K9, M1, [k6, M1] 11 times; rep from *—348 sts.

SIZE 39¾" ONLY

*K1, M1, [k6, M1] 13 times; rep from *—372 sts.

SIZE 43¼" ONLY

*K8, M1 [k5, M1] 15 times; rep from *—396 sts.

SIZE 46¼" ONLY

*K2, M1 [k5, M1] 17 times; rep from *—420 sts.

SIZE 49¾" ONLY

K2, *K4, M1, k5, M1; rep from * to last 2 sts, k2—444 sts.

ALL SIZES

Knit 7 (7, 11, 15, 19, 23) rnds—piece measures about 6¾ (6¾, 7¼, 7½, 8, 8½)" (17 [17, 18.5, 19, 20.5, 21.5] cm) from CO.

Note: *Try on sweater to ensure that the armholes are the desired length. To adjust the fit, work more or fewer MC rnds here; every 4 or 5 rnds added or removed will lengthen or shorten the yoke by about ½" (1.3 cm).*

Divide for Body and Sleeves

Dividing rnd: K50 (55, 60, 65, 70, 75) for half of back, place next 62 (64, 66, 68, 70, 72) sts onto waste-yarn holder for right sleeve, use the backward-loop method (see Glossary) to CO 5 (6, 7, 8, 8, 9) sts, pm for right side "seam," CO 5 (6, 7, 8, 8, 9) more sts, k100 (110, 120, 130, 140, 150) front sts, place next 62 (64, 66, 68, 70, 72) sts onto waste-yarn holder for left sleeve, CO 5 (6, 7, 8, 8, 9) sts, pm for left side "seam," CO 5 (6, 7, 8, 8, 9) more sts, k50 (55, 60, 65, 70, 75) for other half of back—220 (244, 268, 292, 312, 336) body sts; 110 (122, 134, 146, 156, 168) sts each for front and back; rnd still begins at center back.

Body

Work even in St st until piece measures 2½" (6.5 cm) from underarm CO for all sizes.

Body Inc Rnd: *Knit to 1 st before seam m, M1R (see Glossary), k1, slip marker (sl m), k1, M1L (see Glossary); rep from * once more, knit to end—4 sts inc'd.

Cont in St st, rep the Body Inc Rnd every 12 rnds 7 (3, 3, 3, 3, 0) times, then every 16 rnds 2 (5, 3, 3, 3, 4) times, then every 24 rnds 3 (3, 4, 4, 4, 5) times—272 (292, 312, 336, 356, 376) sts; 136 (146, 156, 168, 178, 188) sts each for front and back.

Knit 1 (1, 5, 5, 5, 5) rnd(s) even—piece measures about 23½" (59.5 cm) from dividing rnd for all sizes.

Note: *To adjust body length, work more rnds even with MC until piece measures 3" (7.5 cm) less than desired length.*

Work Rnds 1–3 of Chart A.

Knit 5 rnds with MC.

Work Rnds 13–15 of Chart A.

Knit 5 rnds with MC.

Work Rnds 1–3 of Chart A.

Knit 1 rnd with MC.

Rep the Body Inc Rnd once more—276 (296, 316, 340, 360, 380) sts; 138 (148, 158, 170, 180, 190) sts each for front and back.

Next 4 rnds: *K2, p2; rep from * to end—piece measures about 26½" (67.5 cm) from dividing rnd for all sizes.

Loosely BO all sts in rib patt.

Sleeves

Note: *Sleeves may be worked on dpn or the longest cir needle using the magic-loop method.*

With RS facing, join MC at center of underarm CO sts. Pick up and knit 5 (6, 7, 8, 8, 9) sts across half of underarm CO, k62 (64, 66, 68, 70, 72) held sleeve sts, then pick up and knit 5 (6, 7, 8, 8, 9) sts across rem half of underarm CO sts—72 (76, 80, 84, 86, 90) sts total.

Pm and join for working in rnds.

Inc rnd: Work for your size as foll:

SIZE 32½" ONLY

*K3, M1; rep from *—96 sts.

SIZE 36¼" ONLY

K3, *k4, M1, k3, M1; rep from * to last 3 sts, k3—96 sts.

SIZE 39¾" ONLY

*K4, M1; rep from *—100 sts.

SIZE 43¼" ONLY

*K4, M1, k3, M1; rep from *—108 sts.

SIZE 46¼" ONLY

K4, *k3, M1; rep from * to last 4 sts, k4—112 sts.

SIZE 49¾" ONLY

K1, *k4, M1; rep from * to last st, k1—112 sts.

ALL SIZES

Knit 6 rnds.

Next 4 rnds: *K2, p2; rep from * to end—sleeve measures about 1¼" (3.2 cm) from pick-up rnd.

Loosely BO all sts in rib patt.

Pockets (make two)

With MC and shortest cir needle, CO 34 sts.

Row 1: (WS) P2 *k2, p2; rep from *.

Row 2: (RS) K2, *p2, k2; rep from *.

Rep Rows 1 and 2 once more.

Purl 1 WS row.

Work short-rows as foll:

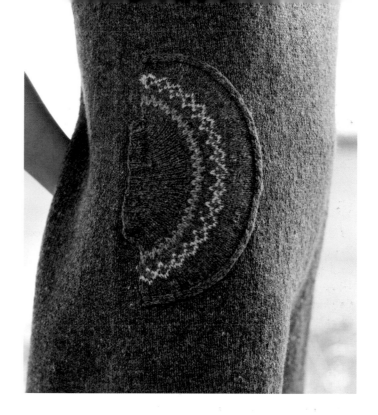

Short-Row 1: (RS) Knit to 8 sts before end of row, wrap next st, turn work.

Short-Row 2: (WS) Purl to 8 sts before end of row, wrap next st, turn work.

Short-Row 3: Knit to previously wrapped st, work wrapped st tog with its wrap, wrap next st, turn work.

Short-Row 4: Purl to previously wrapped st, work wrapped st tog with its wrap, wrap next st, turn work.

Short-Rows 5–14: Rep Short-Rows 3 and 4 five more times, ending with a WS row—only 1 st rem after final wrapped st at each end of needle.

Knit to end of next RS row, working wrapped st tog with its wrap.

Purl 1 WS row across all sts, working final wrapped st tog with its wrap.

Inc Row 1: (RS) K1, M1, *k2, M1; rep from * to last st, k1—51 sts total.

Purl 1 WS row—piece measures about 2½" (6.5 cm) from CO at center.

Work Rows 1–4 of Chart C, ending with a WS row.

Inc Row 2: Working Rnd 5 of Chart C, *k2, M1, k3, M1; rep from * to last st, k1—71 sts.

Work Rows 6–11 of Chart C.

Purl 1 WS row with MC.

Inc Row 3: (RS) *K3, M1, k4, M1; rep from * to last st, k1—91 sts.

Purl 1 WS row—piece measures about 4" (10 cm) from CO at center.

Work short-rows as foll:

Short-Row 1: (RS) Knit to 16 sts before end of row, wrap next st, turn work.

Short-Row 2: (WS) Purl to 16 sts before end of row, wrap next st, turn work.

Short-Row 3: Knit to previously wrapped st, work wrapped st tog with its wrap, k3, wrap next st (4th st after previous wrap), turn work.

Short-Row 4: Purl to previously wrapped st, work wrapped st tog with its wrap, p3, wrap next st (4th st after previous wrap), turn work.

Short-Rows 5 and 6: Rep Short-Rows 3 and 4—7 sts rem after final wrapped st at each end of needle.

Knit to end of next RS row, working wrapped st tog with its wrap.

Purl 1 WS row across all sts, working final wrapped st tog with its wrap—piece measures about 4¾" (12 cm) from CO at center.

Using the I-cord method, BO as foll: With RS facing, use the backward-loop method to CO 3 sts onto left needle tip. *K2, ssk (last I-cord st tog with live pocket st after it), with RS still facing, return 3 sts from right needle onto left needle, bring yarn across back of work; rep from * until all pocket sts have been worked—3 I-cord sts rem.

Return 3 sts to left needle, sl 1, k2tog, psso—1 st rem.

Cut yarn, leaving an 8" (20.5 cm) tail. Thread tail on a tapestry needle, draw through rem st, and pull tight to secure.

Finishing

Soak dress and pockets in cold water with wool wash for at least 20 minutes. Gently squeeze out moisture. Block dress to measurements and block pockets into flat semi-circles. Allow to air-dry completely.

Pin pockets at desired locations, aligning the straight selvedges of each pocket with side "seams" of garment. For the dress shown, the upper edge of each pocket is about 7" (18 cm) down from the dividing rnd. With MC threaded on a tapestry needle, use the mattress stitch (see Glossary) to sew selvedges of pocket to dress, working each seam inward from the I-cord BO to the start of the ribbed section and leaving the ribbed section unattached for pocket opening. Use running sts (see Glossary) to sew the semicircular BO edge of each pocket to the body, sewing in the "ditch" between two I-cord stitch columns for an invisible seam.

Weave in loose ends.

Peerie Weerie Booties

DESIGNED BY
CARRIE BOSTICK
HOGE

In Shetland dialect, *peerie weerie* means "very, very small." Designed with very, very small feet in mind, **Carrie Bostick Hoge** combined a simple four-stitch pattern repeat with a delicate band of stripes to create a pair of booties with the fresh modern look that Carrie is known for. Small though they are, these sweetly patterned booties are perfect for baby's first weeks. Difficult to kick off, they're sure to keep a wee one's tiny toes comfy and warm, no matter what blustery weather rolls in from the sea.

FINISHED SIZE

About 4¼" (11 cm) ankle circumference and 4" (10 cm) foot length.

YARN

Fingering weight (#1 Super Fine).

Shown here: Quince & Co Chickadee (100% North American wool; 181 yd [166 m]/50 g) #152 Kumlien's gull (A; gray), #101 egret (B; natural), and #137 Carrie's yellow (C), 1 skein each.

NEEDLES

Size U.S. 4 (3.5 mm): set of 4 or 5 double-pointed (dpn).

Adjust needle size if necessary to obtain the correct gauge.

NOTIONS

Marker (m); tapestry needle.

GAUGE

26 sts and 32 rnds = 4" (10 cm) in striped St st and charted pattern, worked in rnds.

Bootie (make 2)

With A, use the long-tail method (see Glossary) to CO 28 sts. Divide sts onto 3 dpn so that there are 10 sts on Needle 1, 8 sts on Needle 2, and 10 sts on Needle 3. Place marker (pm) and join for working in rnds, being careful not to twist sts. Rnd begins at center back leg.

Joining B and C as needed, work Rnds 1–21 of Peerie chart, working 4-st patt rep 7 times around—piece measures about 2½" (6.5 cm) from CO.

Shape Foot

Rnds 1 and 2: With B, on Needle 1, knit to last st, k1f&b (see Glossary); on Needle 2, k8; on Needle 3, k1f&b, knit to end—2 sts inc'd in each rnd, 1 st each on Needle 1 and Needle 3.

Rnds 3 and 4: With A, rep Rnds 1 and 2.

Rnds 5–10: Rep Rnds 1–4, then work Rnds 1 and 2 once more—48 sts; 20 sts each on Needle 1 and Needle 3, 8 sts on Needle 2; piece measures about 3¾" (9.5 cm) from CO.

Sole

Change to C and work garter st in rnds as foll:

Rnd 1: Knit.

Rnd 2: Purl.

Rnds 3–8: Rep Rnds 1 and 2 three more times—4 garter ridges total.

Peerie

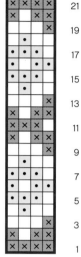

4-st repeat

A

B

C

pattern repeat

Divide sts evenly along center of sole so the first 24 sts of the rnd are on one dpn and the last 24 sts are on another dpn. Hold needles parallel with RS facing tog and WS facing out and use the three-needle method (see Glossary) to BO the sts tog.

Finishing

Weave in loose ends.

Steam-block.

Hap-Lapghan

DESIGNED BY KIRSTEN KAPUR

For a modern take on the traditional, **Kirsten Kapur** designed a square blanket inspired by the everyday *hap* (handknitted; often square) shawls of Shetland. Sized somewhat between a lap robe and afghan, Kirsten's "lapghan" is knitted outward from a few stitches at the center. Bold stripes that graduate in size give movement and depth to the center of the piece and make way for a dynamic chevron border that contrasts nicely with the bold center squares in a uniquely modern design. Worked in a natural-colored wool-alpaca blend, this lofty blanket invites snuggling on cold winter evenings.

FINISHED SIZE

About 45" (114.5 cm) square.

YARN

Worsted weight (#4 Medium).

Shown here: Cascade Yarns Eco Cloud (70% undyed merino wool, 30% undyed baby alpaca; 164 yd [150 m]/100 g): #1810 charcoal (MC), 5 skeins; #1801 cream (CC), 4 skeins.

NEEDLES

Size U.S. 9 (5.5 mm): 24" and 47" (60 and 120 cm) circular (cir) and set of 4 or 5 double-pointed (dpn).

Adjust needle size if necessary to obtain the correct gauge.

NOTIONS

Markers (m); tapestry needle.

GAUGE

14 sts and 27 rnds = 4" (10 cm) in solid-color St st and colorwork patt from Chevron chart, worked in rnds.

stitch guide

Stockinette Stitch with Corner Increases (St st with Incs)

Rnd 1: Knit.

Depending on whether the work is on dpn or a cir needle, work Rnd 2 as foll:

Rnd 2 on dpn: *K1 (corner st), slip marker (sl m), M1L (see Glossary), knit to end of needle, M1R (see Glossary); rep from * for each needle—8 sts inc'd; 2 sts inc'd on each of 4 dpn.

Rnd 2 on cir needle: *K1, sl m, M1L, knit to next m, M1R, sl m; rep from *—8 sts inc'd; 2 sts inc'd at each of 4 sections.

Rep Rnds 1 and 2 for patt, changing colors as given in directions.

notes

○ The center square is worked from the middle outward and is shaped by increasing 2 stitches at each corner every other round.

○ Cut the old yarn when changing to the new color in the striped section, leaving tails long enough to weave in later.

○ When there are too many stitches to fit comfortably on the double-pointed needles, change to the 24" (60 cm) circular needle, keeping the original markers in place and adding a new marker to indicate the end of each double-pointed needle. When there are too many stitches to fit comfortably on the 24" (60 cm) circular needle, change to the 47" (120 cm) needle.

○ When working the chevron pattern, work each M1R or M1L increase into the strand that matches the color of the new stitch you are making.

○ If necessary, use a needle one size larger or smaller for the stranded colorwork section in order to maintain the same gauge as for stockinette stitch.

Lapgahn

With MC, dpn, and using the closed-loop method (see box on page 65), CO 8 sts (2 sts each on 4 needles).

Place marker (pm) and join for working in rnds.

Set-up rnd: *K1 (corner st), pm, M1L (see Glossary), k1, M1R (see Glossary); rep from *—16 sts total; 4 sts on each dpn.

Striped Center Square

Changing needles when necessary (see Notes), work St st with Incs (see Stitch Guide) as foll:

Rnds 1–14: With MC, work Rnds 1 and 2 of patt 7 times—72 sts total; 18 sts on each dpn or each side of square.

Rnds 15–20: With CC, work Rnds 1 and 2 of patt 3 times—96 sts; 24 sts each dpn or side.

Rnds 21–34: With MC, work Rnds 1 and 2 of patt 7 times—152 sts; 38 sts each side.

Rnds 35–42: With CC, work Rnds 1 and 2 of patt 4 times—184 sts; 46 sts each side.

Rnds 43–54: With MC, work Rnds 1 and 2 of patt 6 times—232 sts; 58 sts each side.

Rnds 55–64: With CC, work Rnds 1 and 2 of patt 5 times—272 sts; 68 sts each side.

Rnds 65–74: With MC, work Rnds 1 and 2 of patt 5 times—312 sts; 78 sts each side.

Rnds 75–86: With CC, work Rnds 1 and 2 of patt 6 times—360 sts; 90 sts each side.

Rnds 87–94: With MC, work Rnds 1 and 2 of patt 4 times—392 sts; 98 sts each side.

Rnds 95–108: With CC, work Rnds 1 and 2 of patt 7 times—448 sts; 112 sts each side.

Rnds 109–112: With MC, work Rnds 1 and 2 of patt 2 times—464 sts; 116 sts each side.

Rnd 113: With MC, knit.

Rnd 114: With MC, *k1, sl m, M1L, k57, M1L, k58, M1R, sl m; rep from *—476 sts; 119 sts each side.

Closed-Loop Cast-On

Hold the yarn in your left hand with a 6" (15 cm) tail hanging on the palm side and the yarn wrapped once around your index finger. The working yarn (the yarn coming off the ball of yarn) should be hanging to the back of your hand.

Note: Keep your left index finger inserted in the loop created by this wrap throughout the cast-on.

Step 1: Hold a dpn in your right hand and insert it from front to back into the loop on your left index finger.

Step 2: Wrap the working end of the yarn around the needle as if to knit and draw it through the loop—1 st has been CO (the tail will be wrapped by the CO st).

Step 3: Yo—2 sts CO.

Rep Steps 1–3 until there are 8 sts on the needle (the last st will be a yo; take care not to drop it off the needle).

Step 4: Slide all 8 sts to the other tip of the needle and pull the yarn across the back of the sts (as for working I-cord), [k1, k1 through back loop (k1tbl)] 4 times.

Step 5: Place 2 sts on each of 4 needles and pull on the starting tail to close the hole in the center.

Chevron

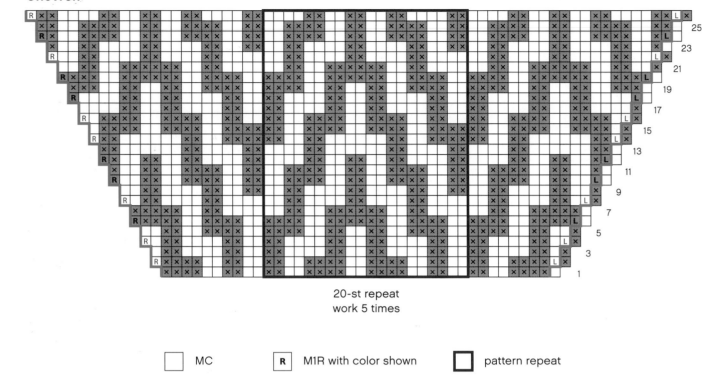

20-st repeat
work 5 times

| | MC | | **R** | M1R with color shown | | ☐ | pattern repeat |
| | CC | | **L** | M1L with color shown | | │ | marker position |

Chevron Border

Next rnd: Establish Rnd 1 of Chevron chart as foll: *Work 1 corner st, sl m, work next 8 sts once, work 20-st patt rep 5 times, work next 10 sts once, sl m; rep from * 3 more times.

Cont as established, work Rnds 2–26 of Chevron chart, inc as shown (see Notes)—580 sts; 145 sts each side.

Garter-Stitch Edging

Rnd 1: With MC, knit.

Rnd 2: With MC, *p1 (corner st), sl m, M1L pwise (see Glossary), purl to next m, M1R pwise (see Glossary), sl m; rep from *—8 sts inc'd; 2 sts each side.

Rnds 3–8: Rep Rnds 1 and 2 three more times—612 sts; 153 sts each side.

With MC, loosely BO all sts.

Finishing

Weave in loose ends.

Block to measurements.

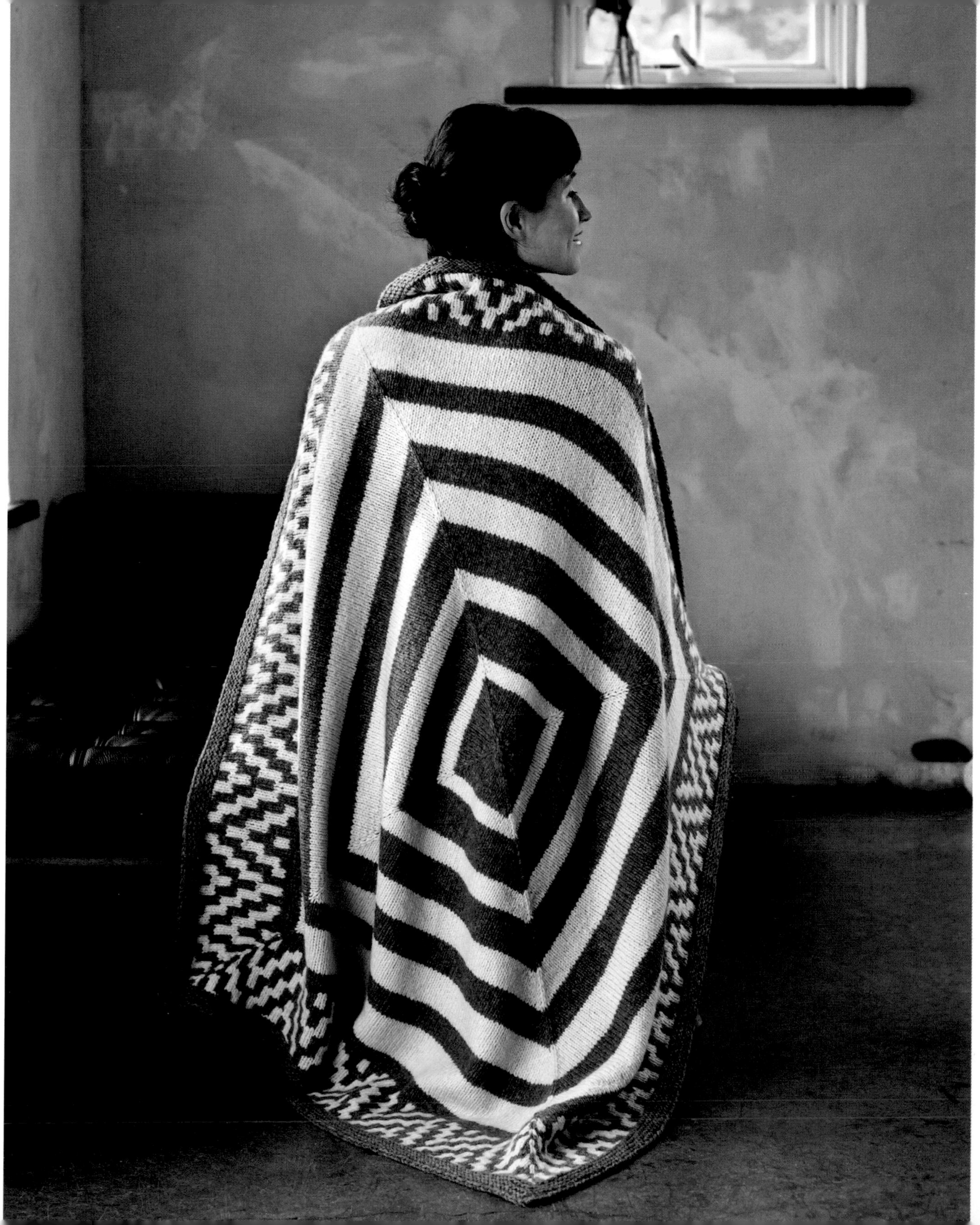

Babsie Bird

DESIGNED BY LUCINDA GUY

Inspired by puffins and other seabirds that flit about the cliffs and meadows in the Shetland Islands, **Lucinda Guy** knitted Babsie, a whimsical three-dimensional bird that will be welcome in any home. The bird is constructed from a number of pieces that are knitted in rows, then sewn together and stuffed with pure sheep's wool. Lucinda used traditional Fair Isle patterns on the wings, body, and tail and accentuated them with cheerful French knots. Knitted in pure Shetland wool yarn with a robust character that has remained unchanged for many decades, Babsie will become firmer, softer, and more durable with time.

FINISHED SIZE

About 13" (33 cm) long from beak tip to tail tip and 5" (12.5 cm) tall.

YARN

Fingering weight (#1 Super Fine).

Shown here: Jamieson & Smith 2-ply Jumper Weight (100% pure Shetland wool; 125 yd [115 m]/ 25 g): #fc34 blue (MC), 2 balls; #202 beige (A), #125 dark orange (B), and #fc7 light orange (C), 1 ball each.

NEEDLES

Size U.S. 2 (2.75 mm): straight or set of 2 double-pointed (dpn).

Adjust needle size if necessary to obtain the correct gauge.

NOTIONS

Stitch holders; tapestry needle; pure wool toy filler or desired stuffing material.

GAUGE

14 sts and 18 rows = 2" (5 cm) in St st before washing (see Notes).

notes

○ The gauge of the finished fabric will be different from the pre-washed fabric because the pieces are washed in warm soapy water and lightly fulled during the finishing process.

○ Add new stitches (shown as plus signs on charts) using either the knitted cast-on or the backward-loop cast-on method (see Glossary); stitches may be cast on at the beginning of a row, at the end of a row, or at both the beginning and end of the same row.

○ Remove stitches by binding off knitwise at start of RS rows or purlwise at start of WS rows.

○ You may find it helpful to use small bobbins or butterflies of colors A, B, and C when working the color patterns.

Right Body

With MC and using the knitted method (see Glossary), CO 39 sts. Work Rows 1–44 of Right Body chart (see page 73), adding and removing sts as shown (see Notes)—52 sts.

Next row: (RS, Row 45 of chart) Work first 31 sts, place sts just worked onto holder, work in patt to end—21 sts rem.

Work Rows 46–55 of chart—4 sts rem. BO all sts.

Left Body

With MC and using the knitted method, CO 39 sts. Work Rows 1–44 of Left Body chart (see page 72), adding and removing sts as shown—53 sts.

Next row: (RS; Row 45 of chart) K2tog, work in patt until there are 21 sts on right needle after BO, use a separate 1 yd (1 m) length of MC to work last 31 sts, then place 31 sts just worked on holder—21 sts rem.

Work Rows 46–55 of chart—4 sts rem. BO all sts.

Head

With A and using the knitted method, CO 3 sts. Work Rows 1–66 of Head chart (see page 75) entirely in solid-color St st with A—3 sts rem. BO all sts.

Note: *The eyes in Rows 27–29 and in Rows 38–40 are added later using duplicate-stitch embroidery.*

Beak

With MC and using the knitted method, CO 11 sts.

Rows 1–5: Work even in St st, beg and ending with a RS row.

Row 6: (WS) CO 1 st, purl to end, CO 1 st—13 sts.

Rows 7–9: Work even.

Row 10: P2tog, purl to last 2 sts, p2tog—11 sts.

Rows 11–13: Work even.

Row 14: P2tog, purl to last 2 sts, p2tog—9 sts.

Rows 15–17: Work even.

Row 18: P2tog, purl to last 2 sts, p2tog—7 sts.

Rows 19 and 20: Work even.

Row 21: K2tog, knit to last 2 sts, k2tog—5 sts.

Row 22: P2tog, p1, p2tog—3 sts rem.

With RS facing, work rem sts as k3tog, then fasten off last st.

Mark the CO edge for the base of the beak, to be sewn to the head later, and mark Row 21 for the tip of the beak.

Right Wing
Wing Front

With MC and using the knitted method, CO 17 sts. Work Rows 1–37 of Right Wing Front chart (see page 75)—3 sts rem. BO all sts.

Wing Backing

Note: The backing for the right wing is worked in solid-color stockinette using the shape from the Left Wing Front chart to produce a mirror-image shape.

With MC and using the knitted method, CO 17 sts. Work Rows 1–37 of Left Wing Front chart (see page 75) entirely with MC, ignoring all colorwork—3 sts rem. BO all sts.

Left Wing
Wing Front

With MC and using the knitted method, CO 17 sts. Work Rows 1–37 of Left Wing Front chart—3 sts rem. BO all sts.

Wing Backing

Note: As for the right wing, the left wing backing is worked in solid-color stockinette using the Right Wing Front chart to create a mirror-image shape.

With MC and using the knitted method, CO 17 sts. Work Rows 1–37 of Right Wing Front chart entirely with MC, ignoring all colorwork—3 sts rem. BO all sts.

Base

With MC and using the knitted method, CO 2 sts.

Row 1 (RS) and Row 2 (WS): Work in St st.

Row 3: CO 1 st, k2, CO 1 st—4 sts.

Row 4: Purl.

Rows 5–7: Rep Rows 3 and 4, then work Row 3 once more—8 sts after Row 7.

Rows 8–31: Work even.

Row 32: K2tog, knit to last 2 sts, k2tog—6 sts.

Row 33: Purl.

Rows 34–37: Rep Rows 32 and 33 two times—2 sts rem after Row 37.

BO all sts.

Finishing
Join Body

Return 31 held sts of right and left body to needles. Hold pieces with RS facing tog and WS facing out and use the three-needle method (see Glossary) to BO the two pieces tog along the top of the back.

Legend

Symbol	Description
☐ MC	
· ☐ A	/ k2tog on RS, p2tog on WS with color shown
✕ B	+ CO 1 st with color shown
Ⅰ C	⌢ BO 1 st with color in use

○ knit with color shown, French knot with A
● knit with color shown, French knot with B
◉ knit with color shown, French knot with C
V knit with A, duplicate st with MC

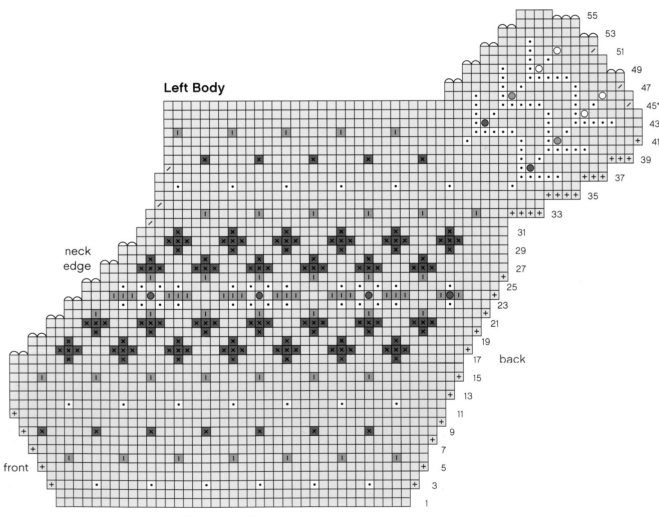

Left Body

neck
edge

front

back

*See instructions.

Right Body

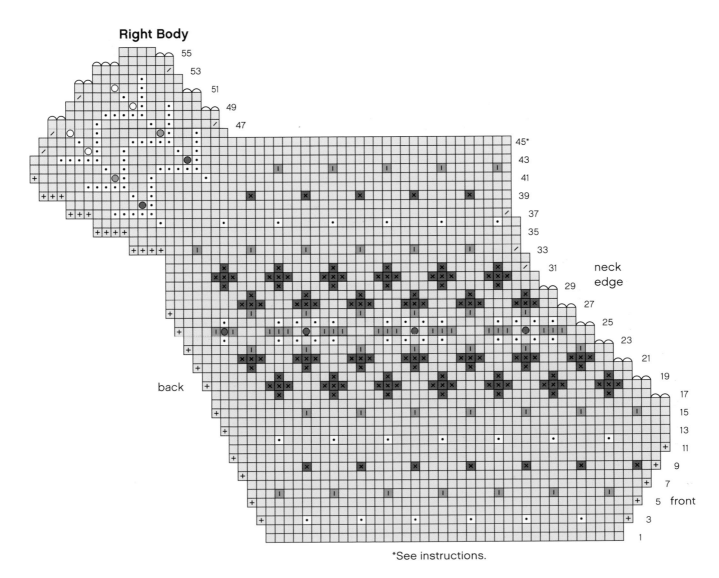

55
53
51
49
47
45*
43
41
39
37
35
33
31
29   neck
27   edge
25
23
21
19
17
15
13
11
9
7
5   front
3
1

back

*See instructions.

Embroidery

Using the charts as a guide, embroider eyes on head with MC and duplicate st embroidery (see Glossary), then work French knots (see Glossary) on body and wing fronts.

Weave in loose ends.

Fulling

Wash all pieces in warm soapy water and rinse well. Gently squeeze out excess moisture by rolling each piece in a towel. Pull into shape and lay flat to dry away from direct heat or sun. Steam-press gently on the WS using a warm iron over a damp cloth.

Assembly

Note: *Fill the bird sufficiently so that it is firm and can stand alone, but not so full that the shapes become distorted.*

Fold the head in half with RS facing tog along the fold line at the top of the head. With RS facing tog, match the fold line in center of head to the three-needle join of the body and pin the neck edge of the head to the neck edge of the body. With MC threaded on a tapestry needle, sew head and body tog.

With RS facing tog, sew beak selvedges tog, leaving CO edge of beak open. Turn beak RS out and stuff with filler.

Sew the front of the head from the fold line at the top of the head toward the body, enclosing the CO edge of the beak in the seam.

Beg at the three-needle back join, sew the right and left bodies tog around the tail and down the back of the body to the CO edges. Turn body RS out.

With RS facing tog, sew each wing front to its backing, leaving the shaped top edge of each wing open. Turn wings RS out and stuff with filler. Close the seam at the top of each wing by sewing into half of each BO st along the shaped top edge.

Pin wings to body as shown in photographs, with upper edge of each wing following the curve of the body/neck seam and leaving about 2" (5 cm) between the wings at the back neck. Sew the wing fronts to the body. Raise each wing and carefully sew the upper edge of the wing backing in the bird's "underarm" to the body to hold the wing in place and prevent it from flapping open too much.

Stuff body with filler.

Pin the base to the body, matching the long selvedges of the base to the CO edges of the right and left body, and sew in place, adding more filler as necessary to achieve a nice, firm shape before closing the last seam.

	☐	MC
	☐ (•)	A
	☒	B
	☐ (I)	C
	╱	k2tog on RS, p2tog on WS with color shown
	+	CO 1 st with color shown
	⌢	BO 1 st with color in use
	○	knit with color shown, French knot with A
	●	knit with color shown, French knot with B
	◉	knit with color shown, French knot with C
	V	knit with A, duplicate st with MC

Right Wing Front

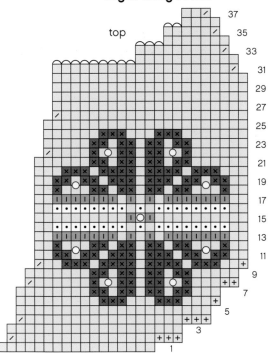

top

37
35
33
31
29
27
25
23
21
19
17
15
13
11
9
7
5
3
1

Left Wing Front

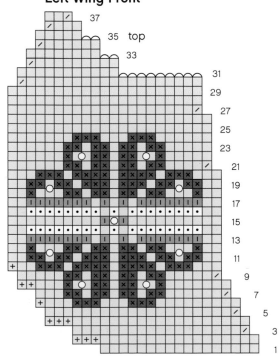

top

37
35
33
31
29
27
25
23
21
19
17
15
13
11
9
7
5
3
1

Head

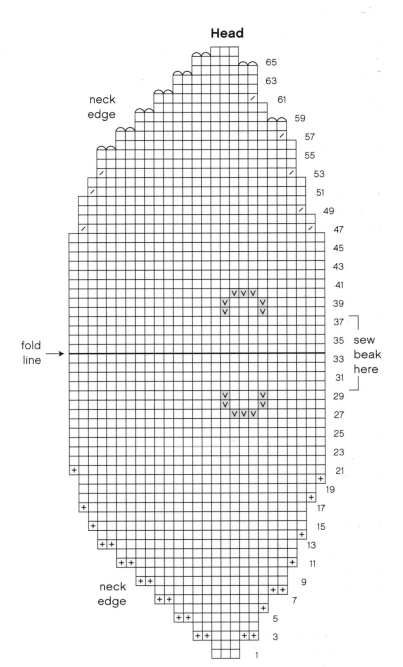

neck edge

65
63
61
59
57
55
53
51
49
47
45
43
41
39
37
35
33
31
29
27
25
23
21
19
17
15
13
11
9
7
5
3
1

fold line →

sew beak here

neck edge

Valenzi Cardigan

DESIGNED BY
MARY JANE
MUCKLESTONE

Inspired by two thick colorwork sweaters from my teenage years—one Cowichan (from the native people of a valley in western Canada) and the other Mexican—I designed a wrap reminiscent of the easy comfort I remember in those roomy sweaters. I chose a local yarn that is minimally processed in natural sheep shades and employed one of the clever shading techniques characteristic of Fair Isle knitting—"peaks," or solid diamond shapes that shade into a wide central area to provide a solid background for a varicolored pattern motif. Worked in rounds with steek stitches that are cut for the center front and sleeves, the pattern is simple to follow and fun to knit!

FINISHED SIZE

About 39 (44¼, 49½)" (99 [112.5, 125.5] cm) bust circumference with 4" (10 cm) front bands overlapped.

Sweater shown measures 39" (99 cm).

Note: This garment is designed to have 3" to 5" (7.5 to 12.5 cm) of positive wearing ease.

YARN

Worsted weight (#4 Medium).

Shown here: Harrisville New England Highland (100% wool; 200 yd [182 m]/100 g): #46 oatmeal (MC), 4 (5, 6) skeins; #47 suede (A; gray-brown), #52 toffee (B; medium brown), #51 walnut (C; dark brown), #49 charcoal (D; charcoal), 1 (1, 2) skein(s) each.

NEEDLES

Ribbing: size U.S. 6 (4 mm): 24" (60 cm) circular (cir) needle and set of 4 or 5 double-pointed (dpn).

Body: size U.S. 8 (5 mm): 24" and 16" (60 and 40 cm) cir needle.

Sleeves and shoulder area: size U.S. 7 (4.5 mm): 16" (40 cm) cir needle and set of 4 or 5 dpn.

Adjust needle size if necessary to obtain the correct gauge.

NOTIONS

Markers (m; one in a unique color), stitch holders or waste yarn; tapestry needle; size G/6 (4 mm) crochet hook or sewing needle and matching thread or sewing machine for securing steeks.

GAUGE

18 sts and 18½ rnds = 4" (10 cm) in Valenzi chart patt with largest needles.

18 sts and 26 rnds = 4" (10 cm) in solid-color stockinette with middle-size needles.

stitch guide

Neck Decreases

Work 4 steek sts, sl m, k2tog, work in patt to last 6 sts, ssk, sl m, work 4 steek sts—2 sts dec'd total; 1 st at each neck edge.

Armhole Decreases

*Work in patt to 2 sts before armhole steek, ssk, sl m, work 8 steek sts, sl m, k2tog; rep from * once more, work in patt to end—4 sts dec'd total; 1 st at each front armhole edge, and 2 back sts.

notes

○ The lower body ribbing is worked back and forth in rows, then the body is joined with center front steek stitches for working in the round to the underarms. The armholes are also steeked; the sleeve stitches are picked up around the armhole openings, then worked in the round down to the ribbed cuffs.

○ The 8-stitch steeks are worked in vertical stripes on two-color rounds. If a round contains only a single color, use that color for all 8 steek stitches.

○ The lower body rounds begin and end in the center of the front steek. Identify the lighter and darker of the two colors in use and work the 4 steek stitches at the start of the round as [dark, light] 2 times. For the 4 steek stitches at the end of the round, work the 4 stitches as [light, dark] 2 times. In this way, the outer stitches of the entire 8-stitch steek are always worked in the lighter color, and the two center stitches of the steek (with the end-of-rnd marker between them) are always worked in the darker color.

○ For each armhole steek, work the 8 steek stitches as [light, dark] 2 times, then [dark, light] 2 times, to keep the outer stitches of the steek in the lighter color and the 2 center stitches of the steek in the darker color.

○ The steeks may be reinforced using the crochet method or with lines of reinforcing stitches sewn by hand or machine.

Body

With MC and 24" (60 cm) cir needle in smallest size, CO 160 (184, 208) sts. Do not join for working in rnds.

Row 1: (RS) K3, *p2, k2, rep from * to last 5 sts, p2, k3.

Row 2: (WS) P3, *k2, p2, rep from * to last 5 sts, k2, p3.

Rep these 2 rows until piece measures 4" (10 cm) from CO, ending with a WS row.

Joining rnd: (RS) Knit to last st, place marker (pm), k1, use the backward-loop method (see Glossary) to CO 3 sts for steek, pm of unique color to indicate center of steek and end-of-rnd, CO 3 more sts, join for working in rnds, k1 (first st of original RS row), pm—166 (190, 214) sts total; the 6 new CO sts and 1 st from each end of the row form the 8-st steek at center front (see Notes).

Next rnd: K36 (41, 46), k2tog, knit to m before front steek, slip marker (sl m), work first 4 steek sts to end at end-of-rnd m in center of front steek—165 (189, 213) sts; 157 (181, 205) body sts; 8 steek sts.

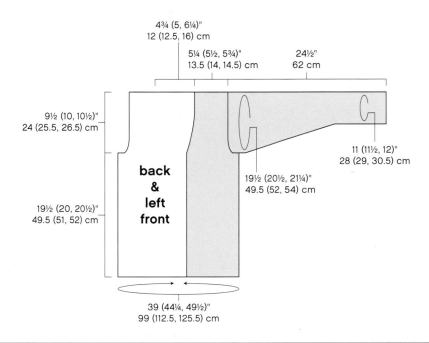

4¾ (5, 6¼)"
12 (12.5, 16) cm

5¼ (5½, 5¾)"
13.5 (14, 14.5) cm

24½"
62 cm

9½ (10, 10½)"
24 (25.5, 26.5) cm

11 (11½, 12)"
28 (29, 30.5) cm

19½ (20½, 21¼)"
49.5 (52, 54) cm

back & left front

19½ (20, 20½)"
49.5 (51, 52) cm

39 (44¼, 49½)"
99 (112.5, 125.5) cm

Change to 24" (60 cm) cir needle in largest size. All rnds now beg and end at m in center of front steek.

Knit 3 (6, 9) rnds even—piece measures 4¾ (5¼, 5¾)" (12 [13.5, 14.5] cm) from CO.

Next rnd: Join A, work 4 steek sts in alternating colors (see Notes), sl m, work Rnd 1 of Valenzi chart (see page 81) over center 157 (181, 205) sts, sl m, work 4 steek sts in alternating colors.

Cont steek sts as established, work Rnds 2–68 of chart— piece measures 19½ (20, 20½)" (49.5 [51, 52] cm) from CO.

Shape Armholes and Neck

Armhole steek rnd: (Rnd 69 of chart) Work 4 steek sts, sl m, work 32 (38, 43) right front sts in established patt, *place the next 9 sts onto stitch holder or waste yarn, pm, use the backward-loop method to CO 8 steek sts in stripe patt (see Notes), pm,* work 75 (87, 101) back sts in patt; rep

from * to * once more for left armhole, work 32 (38, 43) left front sts in patt, work 4 steek sts—163 (187, 211) sts total; 32 (38, 43) sts each front, 75 (87, 101) back sts; 3 steeks with 8 sts each.

Note: *The neck and armholes are shaped at the same time; read all the way through the following sections before proceeding, changing to the shorter cir needle in the largest size when necessary.*

Cont in established patt, dec 1 st at each neck edge (see Stitch Guide) on the next rnd, then every 5th rnd 4 (5, 6) more times—5 (6, 7) sts total removed from each neck edge.

At the same time, dec 1 st at each armhole edge (see Stitch Guide) on the next rnd, then every rnd 2 (4, 6) more times, then every other rnd 0 (2, 3) times—3 (7, 10) sts removed from each front armhole edge and 6 (14, 20) arm- hole sts total removed from back.

When all neck and armhole shaping has been completed 141 (147, 157) sts rem; 24 (25, 26) sts each front, 69 (73, 81) back sts; 3 steeks with 8 sts each.

Cont in patt until Rnd 111 of chart has been completed—armholes measure about 9¼" (23.5 cm) for all sizes. Change to middle-size cir needle and knit 2 (4, 8) rnds with MC—armholes measure 9½ (10, 10½)" (24 [25.5, 26.5] cm).

Next rnd: With MC, BO 4 steek sts, knit to armhole steek, place 24 (25, 26) right front sts just worked on holder or waste yarn, BO 8 steek sts, knit to next armhole steek and place 69 (73, 81) back sts just worked on holder, BO 8 steek sts, knit to front steek and place 24 (25, 26) left front sts just worked on holder, then BO rem 4 steek sts.

Reinforce and Cut Steeks

For all 3 steeks, reinforce each side of the center 2 dark steek sts with slip-stitch crochet or with lines of hand- or machine-stitching (see page 137). With sharp scissors, cut each steek open up the middle, between the 2 dark center sts.

Sleeves

With MC threaded on a tapestry needle, use the Kitchener st (see Glossary) to graft 24 (25, 26) held shoulder sts tog at each side—21 (25, 29) center back neck sts rem on holder.

Note: *Pick up sleeve stitches between the outermost pattern stitch and the adjacent steek stitch.*

With MC, middle-size 16" (40 cm) cir needle, and RS facing, knit across the last 4 held underarm sts, pick up and knit 39 (41, 43) sts evenly spaced to shoulder join, 1 st from join, 39 (41, 43) sts to base of armhole, knit across the first 4 rem held underarm sts, then knit the last held underarm st for a "seam" st, pm and join for working in the rnd—88 (92, 96) sts total.

Knit 4 (6, 8) rnds even—sleeve measures ¾ (1, 1¼)" (2 [2.5, 3.2] cm) from pick-up.

Shape Underarm Gusset

Rnd 1: K3, k2tog, pm for end of gusset, knit to last 6 sts, pm for beg of gusset, ssk, k3, k1 "seam" st—2 sts dec'd.

Rnds 2–4: Knit 3 rnds.

Valenzi

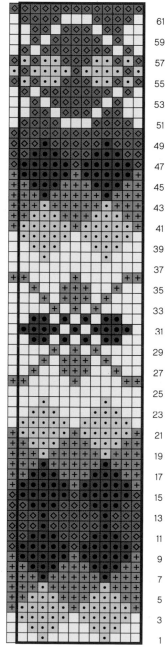

12-st repeat
Work 13 (15, 17) times.

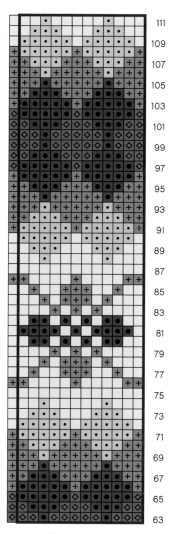

12-st repeat
Work 13 (15, 17) times.

☐ MC	● C
· A	◇ D
+ B	☐ pattern repeat

Rnd 5: K2, k2tog, sl m, knit to m, sl m, ssk, k2, k1 "seam" st—2 sts dec'd.

Rnds 6–8: Knit 3 rnds even.

Rnd 9: K1, k2tog, sl m, knit to m, sl m, ssk, k1, k1 "seam" st—82 (86, 90) sts rem; sleeve measures 2 (2¼, 2½)" (5 [5.5, 6.5] cm) from pick-up rnd.

Taper Sleeve

Knit 3 rnds even, removing gusset m and leaving end-of-rnd m in place.

Dec rnd: K2tog, knit to last 3 sts, ssk, k1 "seam" st—2 sts dec'd.

Cont in St st, rep the dec rnd every 3rd rnd 9 (10, 10) more times, then every 4th rnd 6 (6, 7) times, changing to middle-size dpn when there are too few sts to fit comfortably on cir needle—50 (52, 54) sts rem. Work even until sleeve measures 16½" (42 cm) from pick-up rnd for all sizes.

Next rnd: K2tog 1 (0, 1) time, knit to last 2 (0, 2) sts, k2tog 1 (0, 1) time—48 (52, 52) sts rem.

Cuff

Change to smallest size dpn.

Next rnd: K1, *p2, k2; rep from * to last 3 sts, p2, k1.

Rep this rnd until cuff measures 8" (20.5 cm)—sleeve measures 24½" (62 cm) from pick-up rnd. BO all sts in rib patt.

Finishing

Allow steek sts to roll to inside of garment and whipstitch (see Glossary) in place, if necessary.

Front Bands and Collar

Note: *As for sleeves, pick up front band stitches between the outermost pattern stitch and the adjacent steek stitch.*

With MC, cir needle in smallest size, and beg at lower edge of right front, pick up and knit 137 (142, 146) sts evenly spaced to shoulder join, k21 (23, 29) held back neck sts while inc 1 (1, 3) st(s), then pick up and knit 137 (142, 146) sts evenly spaced along left front to lower edge—296 (308, 324) sts total.

Do not join. Work back and forth in rows as foll:

Row 1: (WS) P3, *k2, p2, rep from * to last 5 sts, k2, p3.

Row 2: (RS) K3, *p2, k2, rep from * to last 5 sts, p2, k3.

Rep these 2 rows until piece measures 4" (10 cm) from pick-up row.

Loosely BO all sts in rib patt.

Weave in loose ends, tidying up joins as you do so. Gently wash garment in lukewarm water with mild soap. Rinse with water of the same temperature. Carefully squeeze out moisture by pressing garment against the sides of the basin. Roll in an absorbent towel to remove excess moisture. Lay flat with front bands overlapped, then fold the collar back, tapering it like a shawl collar so fold ends at the first neckline decrease on each side. Block to measurements (front bands and collar are not shown on the schematic). Fold up cuffs to desired length.

Fara Raglan

DESIGNED BY COURTNEY KELLEY

For this raglan, **Courtney Kelley** paired a traditionally inspired Fair Isle design with retro styling in simple top-down construction. Featuring plain stripes alternating with peerie bands, single rounds of dark brown separate the two, adding a lively punch to the appealing color combination—the sparkling teal blue of a stormy sea illuminated by a ray of light and the tan of windswept grasses close to shore. Courtney keeps the knitting interesting by including a different easy-to-memorize peerie pattern in each peerie band. Worked in a sumptuous blend of baby alpaca, merino, and bamboo, Fara promises to be a luxurious, lively, and enjoyable knit.

FINISHED SIZE

About 32 (36¾, 40, 44¾, 48)" (81.5 [93.5, 101.5, 113.5, 122] cm) bust circumference.

Pullover shown measures 32" (81.5 cm).

YARN

Fingering weight (#1 Extra Fine).

Shown here: The Fibre Company Canopy Fingering (50% baby alpaca, 30% merino, 20% viscose from bamboo; 200 yd [183 m]/50 g): quetzal (MC; teal), 5 (6, 7, 7, 8) skeins; wild ginger (CC1; tan), 2 (2, 2, 3, 3) skeins; sarsaparilla (CC2; brown), conifer (CC3; green), acai (CC4; light red), sumac (CC5; deep purple), plum (CC6; deep rose), laguna (CC7; blue-green), 1 skein each for all sizes.

NEEDLES

Ribbing: size U.S. 1 (2.5 mm): 16" and 24" (40 and 60 cm) circular (cir) and set of 5 double-pointed (dpn).

Body and sleeves: size U.S. 2 (3 mm): 16" and 24" (40 and 60 cm) cir and set of 5 dpn.

Adjust needle size if necessary to obtain the correct gauge.

NOTIONS

Markers (m; one in a unique color); waste-yarn holders; tapestry needle.

GAUGE

30 sts and 34 rnds = 4" (10 cm) in solid-color St st and charted patterns on larger needles, worked in rnds.

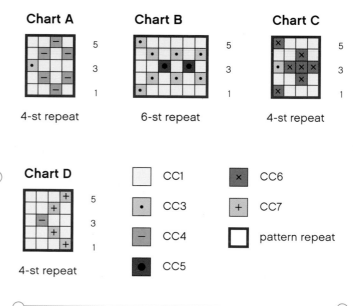

Chart A — 4-st repeat

Chart B — 6-st repeat

Chart C — 4-st repeat

Chart D — 4-st repeat

☐ CC1	✕ CC6	
• CC3	+ CC7	
− CC4	☐ pattern repeat	
● CC5		

notes

○ This pullover is worked in the round from the top down.

○ When increasing for the yoke, change to longer circular needle when there are too many stitches to fit comfortably around the shorter needle.

Yoke

Neckband

With MC and smaller 16" (40 cm) cir needle, CO 140 (140, 152, 152, 164) sts. Place marker (pm) in unique color and join for working in rnds, being careful not to twist sts.

Rib rnd: *K1, p1; rep from *.

Rep the rib rnd until piece measures 1" (2.5 cm) from CO.

Raglan Increases

Set-up rnd: K12 (12, 14, 14, 14) right sleeve sts, pm, k58 (58, 62, 62, 68) front sts, pm, k12 (12, 14, 14, 14) left sleeve sts, pm, k58 (58, 62, 62, 68) back sts.

Rnd begins at right back raglan, at start of right sleeve sts.

Change to larger 16" (40 cm) cir needle.

Rnds 1–5: With MC, *k1, M1 (see Glossary), knit to 1 st before m, M1, k1, slip marker (sl m); rep from * 3 more times—8 sts inc'd in each rnd.

Rnd 6: With CC2, rep Rnd 1—188 (188, 200, 200, 212) sts; 70 (70, 74, 74, 80) sts each for front and back; 24 (24, 26, 26, 26) sts each sleeve.

Rnd 7: With CC1, knit.

Rnds 8–12: Work Rnds 1–5 of Chart A.

Rnd 13: With CC1, knit.

Rnd 14: With CC2, rep Rnd 1—196 (196, 208, 208, 220) sts; 72 (72, 76, 76, 82) sts each for front and back; 26 (26, 28, 28, 28) sts each sleeve.

Rnds 15–19: With MC, rep Rnd 1—8 sts inc'd in each rnd.

Rnd 20: With CC2, rep Rnd 1—8 sts inc'd.

Rnd 21: With CC1, rep Rnd 1—252 (252, 264, 264, 276) sts; 86 (86, 90, 90, 96) sts each for front and back; 40 (40, 42, 42, 42) sts each sleeve.

Rnds 22–26: Work Rnds 1–5 of Chart B.

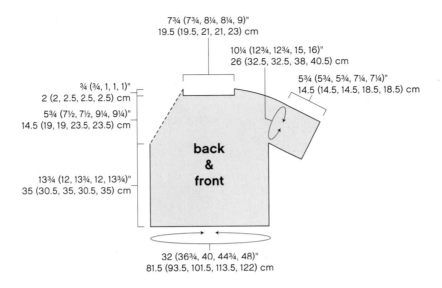

7¾ (7¾, 8¼, 8¼, 9)"
19.5 (19.5, 21, 21, 23) cm

10¼ (12¾, 12¾, 15, 16)"
26 (32.5, 32.5, 38, 40.5) cm

¾ (¾, 1, 1, 1)"
2 (2, 2.5, 2.5, 2.5) cm

5¾ (5¾, 5¾, 7¼, 7¼)"
14.5 (14.5, 14.5, 18.5, 18.5) cm

5¾ (7½, 7½, 9¼, 9¼)"
14.5 (19, 19, 23.5, 23.5) cm

back
&
front

13¾ (12, 13¾, 12, 13¾)"
35 (30.5, 35, 30.5, 35) cm

32 (36¾, 40, 44¾, 48)"
81.5 (93.5, 101.5, 113.5, 122) cm

Rnd 27: With CC1, knit.

Rnd 28: With CC2, rep Rnd 1—8 sts inc'd.

Rnds 29–33: With MC, rep Rnd 1—8 sts inc'd in each rnd.

Rnd 34: With CC2, rep Rnd 1—8 sts inc'd.

Rnd 35: With CC1, rep Rnd 1—316 (316, 328, 328, 340) sts; 102 (102, 106, 106, 112) sts each for front and back; 56 (56, 58, 58, 58) sts each sleeve.

Rnds 36–40: Work Rnds 1–5 of Chart C.

Rnd 41: With CC1, knit.

Rnd 42: With CC2, rep Rnd 1—324 (324, 336, 336, 348) sts; 104 (104, 108, 108, 114) sts each for front and back; 58 (58, 60, 60, 60) sts each sleeve; yoke measures 5" (12.5 cm) from end of neckband rib.

End of Yoke and Lower Body

Cont for your size as foll:

SIZE 32" ONLY

Rnds 43–46: With MC, rep Rnd 1—356 sts; 112 sts each for front and back; 66 sts each sleeve.

Rnd 47: With MC, knit.

Rnd 48: With CC2, knit.

Remove raglan m as you come to them and place new m for side "seams" on next rnd as foll:

Rnd 49: (dividing rnd) With CC1, *k66 sleeve sts and place sts just worked onto holder, use the backward-loop method (see Glossary) to CO 4 underarm sts, pm for side "seam," CO 4 more underarm sts, k112 front sts; rep from * for second sleeve and back—240 sts rem; 120 sts each for front and back; piece measures 5¾" (14.5 cm) from end of neckband rib; rnd begins at right side at start of front sts.

Cont for body as foll:

Rnds 50–54: Work Rnds 1–5 of Chart D.

Rnd 55: With CC1, knit.

Rnd 56: With CC2, knit.

Rnds 57–61: With MC, knit.

Rnd 62: With CC2, knit.

Rnd 63: With CC1, knit.

Rnds 64–68: Work Rnds 1–5 of Chart E.

Rnd 69: With CC1, knit.

Rnd 70: With CC2, knit.

Rnds 71–126: Rep Rnds 57–70 four more times, substituting Chart F in the first rep, Chart G in the second rep, Chart H in the third rep, and Chart I in the fourth rep.

Rnds 127–131: With MC, knit—body measures 9¾" (25 cm) from dividing rnd.

Skip to All Sizes on page 93.

SIZE 36¾" ONLY

Rnds 43–47: With MC, rep Rnd 1—8 sts inc'd in each rnd.

Rnd 48: With CC2, rep Rnd 1—372 sts; 116 sts each for front and back; 70 sts each sleeve.

Rnd 49: With CC1, knit.

Rnds 50–54: Work Rnds 1–5 of Chart D.

Rnd 55: With CC1, knit.

Rnd 56: With CC2, knit.

Rnds 57–61: With MC, rep Rnd 1—412 sts; 126 sts each for front and back; 80 sts each sleeve.

Rnd 62: With CC2, knit.

Remove raglan m as you come to them and place new m for side "seams" on next rnd as foll:

Rnd 63: (dividing rnd) With CC1, *k80 sleeve sts and place sts just worked on holder, use the backward-loop method (see Glossary) to CO 6 underarm sts, pm for side "seam," CO 6 more underarm sts, k156 front sts; rep from * for second sleeve and back—276 sts rem; 138 sts each for front and back; piece measures 7½" (19 cm) from end of neckband rib; rnd begins at right side at start of front sts.

Cont for body as foll:

Rnds 64–68: Work Rnds 1–5 of Chart E.

Rnd 69: With CC1, knit.

Rnd 70: With CC2, knit.

Rnds 71–75: With MC, knit.

Rnd 76: With CC2, knit.

Rnd 77: With CC1, knit.

Rnds 78–82: Work Rnds 1–5 of Chart F.

Rnd 83: With CC1, knit.

Rnd 84: With CC2, knit.

Rnds 85–126: Rep Rnds 71–84 three more times, substituting Chart G in the first rep, Chart H in the second rep, and Chart I in the third rep.

Rnds 127–131: With MC, knit—body measures 8" (20.5 cm) from dividing rnd.

Skip to All Sizes on page 93.

SIZE 40" ONLY

Rnds 43–47: With MC, rep Rnd 1—8 sts inc'd in each rnd.

Rnd 48: With CC2, rep Rnd 1—8 sts inc'd.

Rnd 49: With CC1, rep Rnd 1—392 sts; 122 sts each for front and back; 74 sts each sleeve.

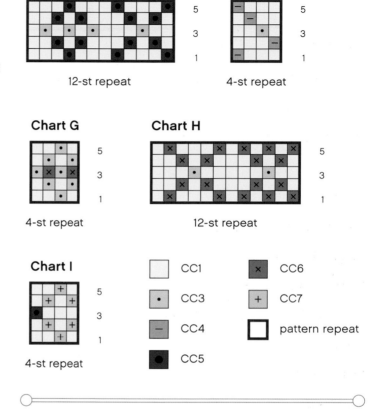

Chart E — 12-st repeat

Chart F — 4-st repeat

Chart G — 4-st repeat

Chart H — 12-st repeat

Chart I — 4-st repeat

CC1 | CC6

CC3 | CC7

CC4 | pattern repeat

CC5

Rnds 50–54: Work Rnds 1–5 of Chart D.

Rnd 55: With CC1, rep Rnd 1—8 sts inc'd.

Rnd 56: With CC2, rep Rnd 1—8 sts inc'd.

Rnds 57 and 58: With MC, rep Rnd 1—424 sts; 130 sts each for front and back; 82 sts each sleeve.

Rnds 59–61: With MC, *knit to end of sleeve sts, sl m, k1, M1, knit to 1 st before m, M1, k1, sl m; rep from * once more for second sleeve and back—4 sts inc'd in each rnd; 2 sts each for front and back; no change to sleeve sts.

Rnd 62: With CC2, rep Rnd 59, inc body sts only—440 sts; 138 sts each for front and back; 82 sts each sleeve.

Remove raglan m as you come to them and place new m for side "seams" on next rnd as foll:

Rnd 63: (dividing rnd) With CC1, *k82 sleeve sts and place sts just worked onto holder, use the backward-loop method (see Glossary) to CO 6 underarm sts, pm for side "seam," CO 6 more underarm sts, k138 front sts; rep from * for second sleeve and back—300 sts rem; 150 sts each for front and back; piece measures 7½" (19 cm) from end of neckband rib; rnd begins at right side at start of front sts.

Cont for body as foll:

Rnds 64–68: Work Rnds 1–5 of Chart E.

Rnd 69: With CC1, knit.

Rnd 70: With CC2, knit.

Rnds 71–75: With MC, knit.

Rnd 76: With CC2, knit.

Rnd 77: With CC1, knit.

Rnds 78–82: Work Rnds 1–5 of Chart F.

Rnd 83: With CC1, knit.

Rnd 84: With CC2, knit.

Rnds 85–140: Rep Rnds 71–84 four more times, substituting Chart G in the first rep, Chart H in the second rep, Chart I in the third rep, and Chart A in the fourth rep.

Rnds 141–145: With MC, knit—body measures 9¾" (25 cm) from dividing rnd.

Skip to All Sizes on page 93.

SIZE 44¾" ONLY

Rnds 43–47: With MC, rep Rnd 1—8 sts inc'd in each rnd.

Rnd 48: With CC2, rep Rnd 1—8 sts inc'd.

Rnd 49: With CC1, rep Rnd 1—392 sts; 122 sts each for front and back; 74 sts each sleeve.

Rnds 50–54: Work Rnds 1–5 of Chart D.

Rnd 55: With CC1, rep Rnd 1—8 sts inc'd.

Rnd 56: With CC2, rep Rnd 1—8 sts inc'd.

Rnds 57–61: With MC, rep Rnd 1—8 sts inc'd in each rnd.

Rnd 62: With CC2, rep Rnd 1—456 sts; 138 sts each for front and back; 90 sts each sleeve.

Rnd 63: With CC1, knit.

Rnds 64–68: Work Rnds 1–5 of Chart E (see page 89).

Rnd 69: With CC1, rep Rnd 1—8 sts inc'd.

Rnd 70: With CC2, rep Rnd 1—8 sts inc'd.

Rnd 71: With MC, rep Rnd 1—480 sts; 144 sts each for front and back; 96 sts each sleeve.

Rnd 72: With MC, *knit to end of sleeve sts, sl m, k1, M1, knit to 1 st before m, M1, k1, sl m; rep from * once more for second sleeve and back—4 sts inc'd; 2 sts each for front and back; no change to sleeve sts.

Rnds 73–75: With MC, rep Rnd 72, inc body sts only—496 sts; 152 sts each for front and back; 96 sts each sleeve.

Rnd 76: With CC2, knit.

Remove raglan m as you come to them and place new m for side "seams" on next rnd as foll:

Rnd 77: (dividing rnd) With CC1, *k96 sleeve sts and place sts just worked onto holder, use the backward-loop

method (see Glossary) to CO 8 underarm sts, pm for side "seam," CO 8 more underarm sts, k144 front sts; rep from * for second sleeve and back—336 sts; 168 sts each for front and back; piece measures 9¼" (23.5 cm) from end of neckband rib; rnd begins at right side at start of front sts.

Cont for body as foll:

Rnds 78–82: Work Rnds 1–5 of Chart F.

Rnd 83: With CC1, knit.

Rnd 84: With CC2, knit.

Rnds 85–89: With MC, knit.

Rnd 90: With CC2, knit.

Rnd 91: With CC1, knit.

Rnds 92–96: Work Rnds 1–5 of Chart G.

Rnd 97: With CC1, knit.

Rnd 98: With CC2, knit.

Rnds 99–140: Rep Rnds 85–98 three more times, substituting Chart H in the first rep, Chart I in the second rep, and Chart A in the third rep.

Rnds 141–145: With MC, knit—body measures 8" (20.5 cm) from dividing rnd.

Skip to All Sizes on page 93.

SIZE 48" ONLY

Rnds 43–47: With MC, rep Rnd 1—8 sts inc'd in each rnd.

Rnd 48: With CC2, rep Rnd 1—8 sts inc'd.

Rnd 49: With CC1, rep Rnd 1—404 sts; 128 sts each for front and back; 74 sts each sleeve.

Rnds 50–54: Work Rnds 1–5 of Chart D.

Rnd 55: With CC1, rep Rnd 1—8 sts inc'd.

Rnd 56: With CC2, rep Rnd 1—8 sts inc'd.

Rnds 57–61: With MC, rep Rnd 1—8 sts inc'd in each rnd.

Rnd 62: With CC2, rep Rnd 1—468 sts; 144 sts each for front and back; 90 sts each sleeve.

Rnd 63: With CC1, knit.

Rnds 64–68: Work Rnds 1–5 of Chart E (see page 89).

Rnd 69: With CC1, rep Rnd 1—8 sts inc'd.

Rnd 70: With CC2, rep Rnd 1—8 sts inc'd.

Rnds 71–73: With MC, rep Rnd 1—508 sts; 154 sts each for front and back; 100 sts each sleeve.

Rnds 74 and 75: With MC, *knit to end of sleeve sts, sl m, k1, M1, knit to 1 st before m, M1, k1, sl m; rep from * once more for second sleeve and back—4 sts inc'd in each rnd; 2 sts each for front and back; no change to sleeve sts.

Rnd 76: With CC2, rep Rnd 74, inc body sts only—520 sts; 160 sts each for front and back; 100 sts each sleeve.

Remove raglan m as you come to them and place new m for side "seams" on next rnd as foll:

Rnd 77: (dividing rnd) With CC1, *k100 sleeve sts and place sts just worked onto holder, use the backward-loop method (see Glossary) to CO 10 underarm sts, pm for side "seam," CO 10 more underarm sts, k160 front sts; rep from * for second sleeve and back—360 sts; 180 sts each for front and back; piece measures 9¼" (23.5 cm) from end of neckband rib; rnd begins at right side at start of front sts.

Cont for body as foll:

Rnds 78–82: Work Rnds 1–5 of Chart F.

Rnd 83: With CC1, knit.

Rnd 84: With CC2, knit.

Rnds 85–89: With MC, knit.

Rnd 90: With CC2, knit.

Rnd 91: With CC1, knit.

Rnds 92–96: Work Rnds 1–5 of Chart G.

Rnd 97: With CC1, knit.

Rnd 98: With CC2, knit.

Rnds 99–154: Rep Rnds 85–98 four more times, substituting Chart H in the first rep, Chart I in the second, Chart A in the third, and Chart B in the fourth.

Rnds 155–159: With MC, knit—body measures 9¾" (25 cm) from dividing rnd.

ALL SIZES

Change to smaller cir needle.

Rib rnd: *K1, p1; rep from *.

Rep the rib rnd for 4" (10 cm) or to desired length—body measures 13¾ (12, 13¾, 12, 13¾)" (35 [30.5, 35, 30.5, 35] cm) from dividing rnd and 19½ (19½, 21¼, 21¼, 23)" (49.5 [49.5, 54, 54, 58.5] cm) total from end of neckband rib.

Loosely BO all sts in rib patt.

Sleeves

Note: *The sleeves are worked in pattern to match the body, beginning with Rnd 1 of Chart D (E, E, F, F). Depending on your size, the number of stitches picked up along the underarm may not exactly equal the underarm CO stitches because the total number of sleeves stitches must be a multiple of 4 (12, 12, 4, 4) to accommodate full repeats of Chart D (E, E, F, F).*

Place 66 (80, 82, 96, 100) held sleeve sts onto larger dpn and, with RS facing, join yarns for Rnd 1 of Chart D (E, E, F, F) to center of underarm CO sts.

Rnd 1: Working according to chart patt, pick up and knit 5 (8, 7, 8, 10) sts along first half of underarm CO, work 66 (80, 82, 96, 100) sts in patt, pick up and knit 5 (8, 7, 8, 10) sts along other half of underarm CO—76 (96, 96, 112, 120) sts total.

Rnds 2–5: Work Rnds 2–5 of chart.

Rnd 6: With CC1, knit.

Rnd 7: With CC2, knit.

Rnds 8–12: With MC, knit.

Rnd 13: With CC2, knit.

Rnd 14: With CC1, knit.

Rnds 15–19: Work Rnds 1–5 of next chart in sequence to match body.

Rep Rnds 6–19 one (one, one, two, two) more times, ending with Rnd 5 of the final chart.

With CC1, knit 1 rnd.

With CC2, knit 1 rnd.

With MC, knit 1 rnd—36 (36, 36, 50, 50) rnds total; sleeve measures 4¼ (4¼, 4¼, 5¾, 5¾)" (11 [11, 11, 14.5, 14.5] cm).

Change to smaller dpn.

Rib rnd: *K1, p1; rep from *.

Rep the rib rnd for 1½" (3.8 cm)—sleeve measures 5¾ (5¾, 5¾, 7¼, 7¼)" (14.5 [14.5, 14.5, 18.5, 18.5] cm).

Loosely BO all sts in rib patt.

Finishing

Weave in loose ends.

Block to measurements.

Mud Cloth Bag

DESIGNED BY MAGS KANDIS

Mags Kandis delights in tossing ethnic elements into otherwise casual modern looks. Here, her point of departure is the intricate, high-contrast geometric patterns found on traditional mud cloth from Mali. The resulting bag, with its clean sculptural birch handles, blends African and modern Scandinavian influences with a whisper of the traditional allover patterning characteristic of Fair Isle knitting. For an unexpected burst of color, Mags lined the bag with shocking pink silk that offers a bright and secret surprise. Mags knitted the bag shown here in rows, but you could work most of it in rounds if you prefer.

FINISHED SIZE

About 17" (43 cm) wide and 16¼" (41.5 cm) tall, excluding handles.

YARN

DK weight (#3 Light).

Shown here: Classic Elite Woodland (65% wool, 35% nettles; 131 yd [120 m]/50 g): #3175 charcoal (MC), 3 balls; #3101 ivory (CC), 2 balls.

NEEDLES

Size U.S. 6 (4 mm): straight or 24" (60 cm) circular (cir).

Adjust needle size if necessary to obtain the correct gauge.

NOTIONS

Tapestry needle; ½ yd (.46 m) lining fabric; sharp-point sewing needle and matching thread; one pair of D-shaped wooden handles about 6¾" (17 cm) wide (handles shown are #hw13 from Tall Poppy Craft Products, www .tallpoppycraft.com).

GAUGE

22 sts and 22 rows/rnds = 4" (10 cm) in charted pattern.

Bag Sides (make 2)

With MC, CO 95 sts (see Notes).

Work Rows 1–60 of Mud Cloth chart, ending with a WS row.

Shape Sides

Dec as shown on chart, work Rows 61–81—73 sts rem.

Work Rows 82–94 of chart—piece measures about 17" (43 cm) from CO. Cut CC.

Next row: (RS) With MC, k1, *k2tog; rep from *—37 sts rem.

BO all sts knitwise.

Make a second piece the same as the first.

Finishing

Weave in loose ends. Block to measurements.

Assembly

With yarn threaded on a tapestry needle, sew the pieces tog along their CO edges for the bottom of the bag, then sew the sides tog to the start of the shaping at Row 61.

Using the bag as a template, cut out two lining pieces with ½" (1.3 cm) seam allowances at the sides and across the bottom. With RS of fabric facing tog, sew bottom and sides of lining. Turn lining right side out, fold raw edges of shaped sides and top ½" (1.3 cm) to WS and press.

Insert lining into bag so that wrong sides of bag and lining face tog. With sharp-point sewing needle and matching thread, sew lining in place along shaped edges, leaving last 12 rows at top of bag free for attaching the handles.

Fold top 12 rows around handles and stitch firmly in place using yarn threaded on a tapestry needle.

Stitch top of lining to BO edge of bag.

Mud Cloth

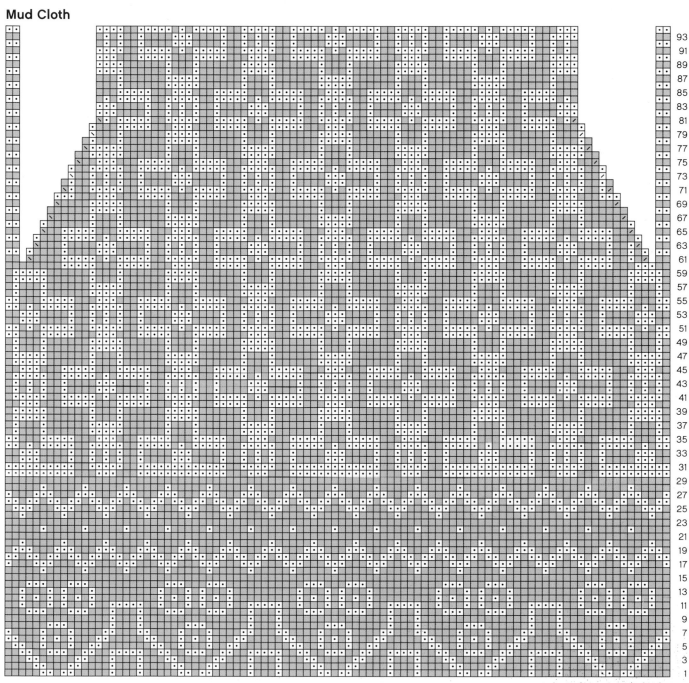

93
91
89
87
85
83
81
79
77
75
73
71
69
67
65
63
61
59
57
55
53
51
49
47
45
43
41
39
37
35
33
31
29
27
25
23
21
19
17
15
13
11
9
7
5
3
1

95 sts dec'd to 73 sts

	MC		• CC		/ k2tog with color shown		\ k2tog tbl with color shown

Mareel Shrug

DESIGNED BY NORAH GAUGHAN

An example of her ingenious construction techniques, **Norah Gaughan's** geometric shrug is mostly seamless. For each sleeve, she knitted a pentagon and added a sixth section that wraps around to form the front. Stitches for the back are picked up along the edges of these pieces and decreased at regular intervals to form a hexagon, ending with just a few stitches in the center. All that's left to finish are the shoulder seams and two decorative buttons on the front. For the Fair Isle bands, Norah chose glowing pattern colors that contrast beautifully with the soft neutral of the sweater body.

FINISHED SIZE

About 40" (101.5 cm) bust circumference, with front points overlapped about 2" (5 cm).

YARN

Sportweight (#2 Fine).

Shown here: Berroco Ultra Alpaca Light (50% super fine alpaca, 50% Peruvian wool; 144 yd [133 m]/50 g): #4204 buckwheat (MC, brown), 4 skeins; #4245 pitch black (A), 2 skeins; #4215 star sapphire (B), #4217 tupelo (C; gold), and #4209 moonshadow (D; light gray), 1 skein each.

NEEDLES

Ribbing: size U.S. 3 (3.25 mm): 32" (80 cm) circular (cir).

Body: size U.S. 5 (3.75 mm): 32" (80 cm) cir and set of 4 or 5 double-pointed (dpn).

Adjust needle size if necessary to obtain the correct gauge.

NOTIONS

Markers (m); tapestry needle; two ⅞" (2.2 cm) buttons; size F/5 (3.75 mm) crochet hook.

GAUGE

23 sts and 26 rows = 4" (10 cm) in solid-color St st and colorwork patt from charts.

- Each of the two identical front/sleeve pieces is worked back and forth in rows and is made up of six sections: five sections that would normally form a flat pentagon, plus an additional sixth section the same size as the other five. Each more-than-a-full-pentagon piece is folded to form a front, sleeve, and side.

- The back hexagon is worked in the round from the outside toward the center. It begins by picking up stitches along the edges of the front/sleeve pieces for four sides of the hexagon, while casting on stitches for the remaining two sides across the back neck and lower back edges. This leaves only two shoulder seams to be sewn during finishing.

Front/Sleeve (make 2)

With MC and smaller cir needle, CO 362 sts. Do not join for working in rnds.

Work in rows as foll:

Set-up row: (WS) P1, *place marker (pm), p1, [k2, p2] 14 times, k2, p1; rep from * 5 more times, p1—60 sts each in 6 marked sections; 1 selvedge st each side.

Row 1: (RS) K1, *ssk, work in established rib (knit the knits and purl the purls as they appear) to 2 sts before next m, k2tog; rep from * 5 more times, k1—12 sts dec'd; 2 sts dec'd from each marked section.

Rows 2 and 4: P1, work in established rib to last st, p1.

Row 3: K1, work in established rib to last st, k1.

Row 5: Rep Row 1—338 sts rem; 56 sts each in 6 marked sections; 1 selvedge st each side.

Row 6: Rep Row 2—piece measures about 1" (2.5 cm) from CO.

Change to larger cir needle.

Next row: (RS) Establish patt from Front/Sleeve chart (see page 102) as foll: K1, sl m, *work Row 1 of chart over 56 sts while dec them to 54 sts as shown, sl m; rep from * 5 more times, k1—326 sts; 54 sts each in 6 marked sections; 1 selvedge st at each side.

Work Rows 2–50 of chart, working selvedge sts in St st to match the color of the adjacent chart st—14 sts rem; 2 sts each in 6 marked sections, 1 selvedge st each side; each section measures about 8¾" (22 cm) from CO, measured straight up the center, and about 10½" (26.5 cm) from CO measured along a diagonal decrease line.

Cut yarn, leaving a 6" (15 cm) tail. Thread tail on a tapestry needle and draw through rem sts. Pull tail snugly to draw sts tog and secure on WS.

Make a second front/sleeve the same as the first.

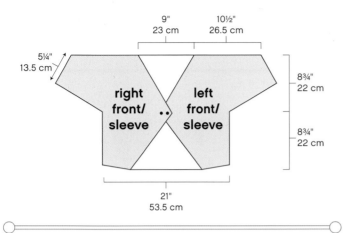

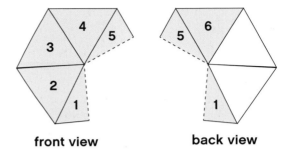

Figure 1
Left front/sleeve folding diagram.

Back

Fold Front/Sleeve Pieces

With RS facing, think of the 6 sections of the left front/sleeve piece as being numbered from Section 1 at the beg of RS rows through Section 6 at the end of RS rows; you may find it helpful to pin scrap paper numbers to each section. Fold the piece down the center of Section 5 with WS touching and RS facing out, then fold the piece in the same manner down the center of Section 1. With the front facing you, the left front/sleeve will look like the front view in **Figure 1**. Maintaining the folded shape, flip the piece over so its other side is facing you and the piece is oriented as shown in the back view of **Figure 1**.

As for the left front/sleeve, think of the 6 sections of the right front/sleeve piece as being numbered from Section 1 at the beg of RS rows through Section 6 at the end of RS rows. Fold the piece down the center of Section 2 with WS touching and RS facing out, then fold the piece in the same manner down the center of Section 6. With the front facing you, the right front/sleeve will look like the front view in **Figure 2**. Maintaining the folded shape, flip the piece over so its other side is facing you and the piece is oriented as shown in the back view of **Figure 2**.

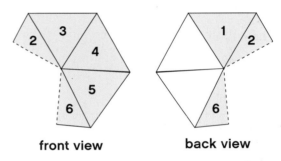

Figure 2
Right front/sleeve folding diagram.

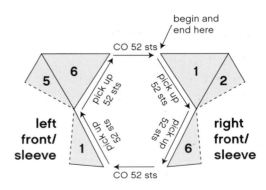

Figure 3
Back hexagon pick-up and CO diagram.

Front/Sleeve

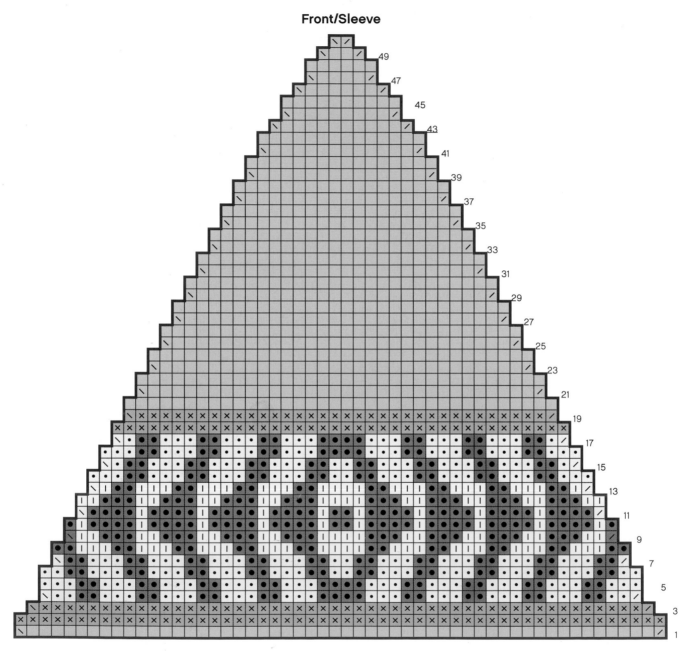

49
47
45
43
41
39
37
35
33
31
29
27
25
23
21
19
17
15
13
11
9
7
5
3
1

56-st repeat
dec'd to 2-st repeat
work 6 times

Back

MC
A
B
C
D

k2tog on RS rows and all rnds;
p2tog on WS rows with color shown

ssk on RS rows and all rnds;
ssp on WS rows with color shown

pattern repeat

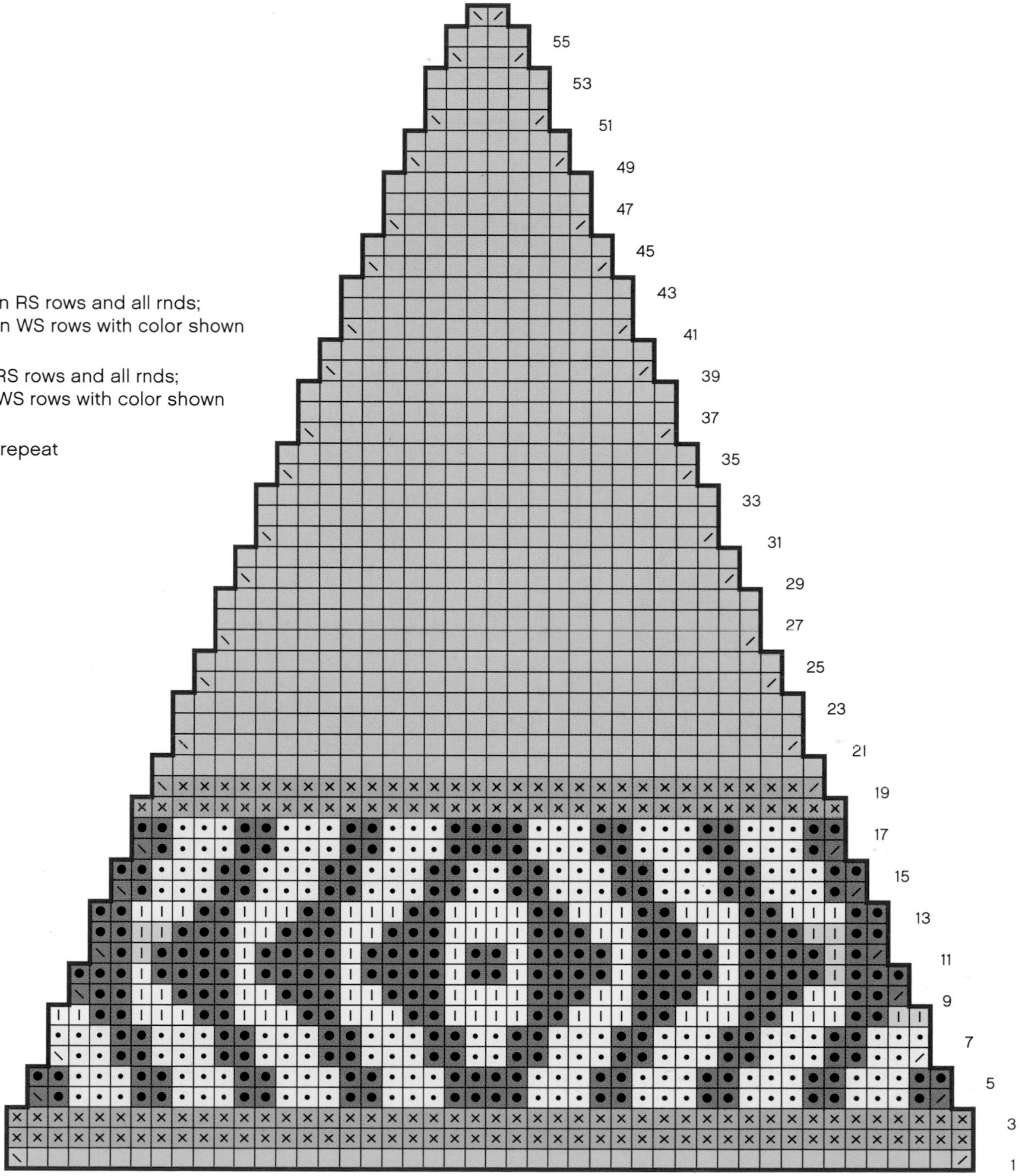

55
53
51
49
47
45
43
41
39
37
35
33
31
29
27
25
23
21
19
17
15
13
11
9
7
5
3
1

48-st repeat dec'd to 2-st repeat
work 6 times

Back Hexagon

Arrange the two front/sleeve pieces as shown in **Figure 3** (only the RS of each piece is shown).

With MC, smaller cir needle, and RS facing, pick up and knit 52 sts along the selvedge of Section 1 of right front/sleeve, pm, pick up and knit 52 sts along the selvedge of Section 6 of right front/sleeve, pm, use the backward-loop method (see Glossary) to CO 52 sts across lower back, pm, pick up and knit 52 sts along the selvedge of Section 1 of left front/sleeve, pm, pick up and knit 52 sts along the selvedge of Section 6 of left front/sleeve, pm, use the backward-loop method to CO 52 sts across back neck, pm, and join for working in rnds—312 sts total; 52 sts each in 6 marked sections.

Rnd 1: *K1, [p2, k2] 12 times, p2, k1, sl m; rep from * 5 more times.

Rnd 2: *Ssk, work in established rib to 2 sts before next m, k2tog, sl m; rep from * 5 more times—12 sts dec'd; 2 sts dec'd from each marked section.

Rnds 3 and 5: Work in established rib.

Rnd 4: K1, work in rib as established to last st, k1.

Rnd 6: Rep Rnd 2—288 sts; 48 sts each in 6 marked sections.

Rnd 7: Work in established rib—piece measures about 1" (2.5 cm) from pick-up/CO.

Change to larger cir needle.

Next rnd: Establish patt from Back chart as foll: *Work Rnd 1 of chart over 48 sts while dec them to 46 sts as shown, sl m; rep from * 5 more times—276 sts; 46 sts each in 6 marked sections.

Work Rnds 2–56 of chart, changing to dpn when there are too few sts to fit comfortably on cir needle—12 sts rem;

2 sts each in 6 marked sections; each section measures about 9½" (24 cm) from pick-up/CO measured straight up the center and about 10½" (26.5 cm) from pick-up/CO measured along a diagonal decrease line.

Cut yarn, leaving a 6" (15 cm) tail. Thread tail on a tapestry needle and draw through rem sts, pull tight to close hole, and secure on WS.

Finishing

Lay garment flat so RS of fronts are facing you with pieces oriented as shown in schematic.

For right front/sleeve, use MC threaded on a tapestry needle to sew CO edge of Section 3 to CO edge of Section 1 for right shoulder seam. For left front/sleeve, use MC threaded on a tapestry needle to sew CO edge of Section 4 to CO edge of Section 6 for left shoulder seam.

With MC, crochet hook, RS facing, and beg at left shoulder seam, work 1 row of reverse single crochet (see Glossary) across back neck to prevent stretching, ending at right shoulder seam.

Weave in loose ends.

Overlap right front point over left front point by about 2" (5 cm) or where desired fit is achieved, and sew two buttons to RS of overlap as shown, sewing through both layers of fabric.

Squirrel-in-the-Woods Mittens

DESIGNED BY ELLI STUBENRAUCH

No land mammals are native to Shetland, but **Elli Stubenrauch** found a way to introduce a stealth squirrel into her mittens. Beginning with a short section of scalloped corrugated ribbing that grades into an allover tree pattern, a squirrel is added to one mitten with duplicate stitches (you could just as easily add a bird or some other animal). Elli used side-seam thumb gussets that allow the mittens to be worn with equal comfort on either hand—display the squirrel on the palm of one hand or the back of the other. Knitted with worsted-weight wool at a dense gauge, these mittens will protect your hands from gale-force winds.

FINISHED SIZE
About 8¾" (22 cm) hand circumference and 10¼" (26 cm) long.

YARN
Worsted weight (#4 Medium).

Shown here: Green Mountain Spinnery Wonderfully Woolly (100% wool; 250 yd [229 m]/4 oz [114 g]): natural grey (MC), fiddlehead (CC1; green), and black walnut (CC2; dark brown), 1 skein each.

Note: Only a few yards (meters) of CC2 are required.

NEEDLES
Size U.S. 4 (3.5 mm): set of 5 double-pointed (dpn).

Adjust needle size if necessary to obtain the correct gauge.

NOTIONS
Marker (m); waste yarn for holding sts; tapestry needle.

GAUGE
22 sts and 26 rnds = 4" (10 cm) in charted patts, worked in rnds (see Notes).

stitch guide

Right Half-Duplicate St

Embroider as for regular duplicate stitch (see Glossary), but only over the right half of the knit stitch "V."

Left Half-Duplicate St

Embroider as for regular duplicate stitch (see Glossary), but only over the left half of the knit stitch "V."

notes

○ This project is deliberately worked at a denser gauge than is typical for worsted-weight yarn.

○ There are two colors used in every round so there will always be two strands between the needles to choose from when you work a M1R or M1L increase (see Glossary). Work each increase into the strand that matches the color of the new stitch you are making.

Mitten with All Trees

With MC, CO 48 sts. Arrange sts evenly on 4 dpn (12 sts on each needle), place marker (pm), and join for working in rnds, being careful not to twist sts.

Cuff

Join CC1.

Rnds 1–5: *With both colors in back, k1 with CC1, bring the MC to the front and p1 with MC, then bring the MC to the back again; rep from *—piece measures about 1" (2.5 cm) from CO.

Note: *The unused color should always be stranded across the WS of the work.*

Hand

Work Rnds 1–32 of Chart A, working incs for thumb gusset as shown (see Notes)—66 sts.

Next rnd: (Rnd 33 of chart) Work first 9 sts of rnd and inc them to 10 sts as shown, then place 10 sts just worked and last 9 sts of previous rnd onto a waste-yarn holder, work to end of rnd—48 sts rem; 19 thumb sts on holder.

Chart A

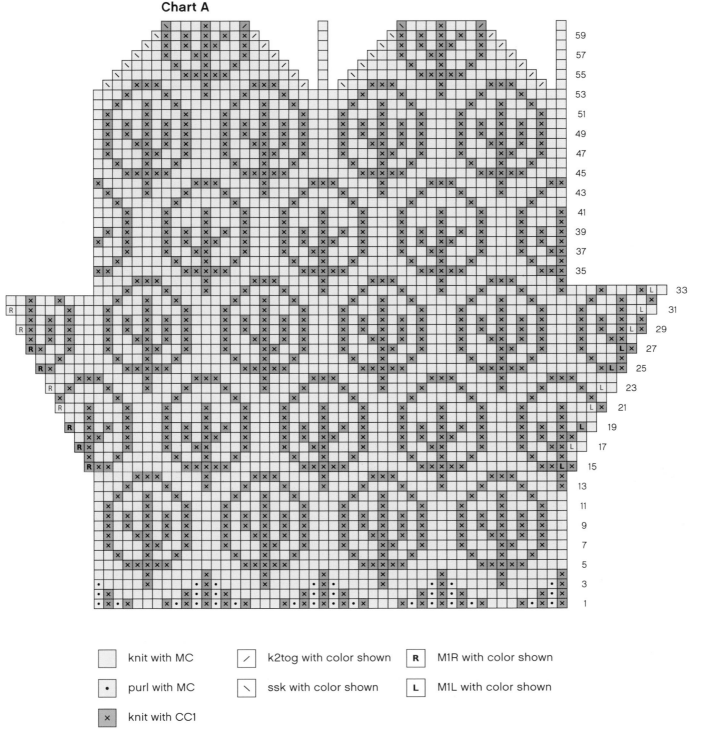

knit with MC
purl with MC
knit with CC1
k2tog with color shown
ssk with color shown
M1R with color shown
M1L with color shown

Work Rnds 34–60 of chart, dec as shown—20 sts rem.

Cut yarn, leaving an 18" (45.5 cm) tail of MC. Place first 10 sts onto one waste-yarn holder and rem 10 sts onto a second waste-yarn holder. Turn mitten inside out. Return held sts to separate needles and use the MC tail and the three-needle method (see Glossary) to BO sts tog; the BO welt will be on the inside of the mitten.

Turn mitten right side out again.

Thumb

Return 19 held thumb sts onto 3 dpn as evenly distributed as possible. Join yarns to beg of sts with RS facing, leaving an 8" (20.5 cm) tail of MC for closing any gaps later.

Partial rnd: Work Rnd 1 of Thumb chart over first 9 sts, inc 1 st as shown on chart, pm and join for working in rnds—20 sts total; thumb rnds now beg and end at the outer edge of thumb; not in the crease between the thumb and hand.

Work Rnds 2–9 of chart, working incs and decs as indicated—16 sts rem.

Next rnd: With MC, [k2tog] 8 times—8 sts rem.

Cut yarn, leaving a 6" (15 cm) tail of MC. Thread tail on a tapestry needle, draw through rem sts, pull tight to close hole, and fasten off on WS.

Thumb

Mitten with Squirrel and Trees

Work as for mitten with all trees, except substitute Chart B. Knit any CC2 sts for the squirrel with MC; the squirrel will be added later with embroidery.

Finishing

With CC2, use duplicate sts and half-duplicate sts (see Stitch Guide and Glossary) to embroider squirrel motif as shown in Chart B.

Weave in loose ends, using MC tail at start of each thumb to close gaps between thumb and hand.

Block to measurements.

Chart B

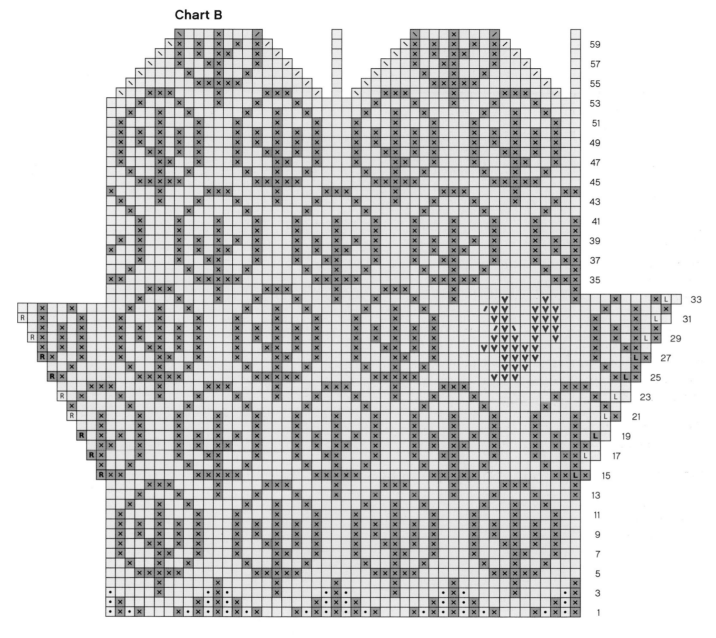

59
57
55
53
51
49
47
45
43
41
39
37
35
33
31
29
27
25
23
21
19
17
15
13
11
9
7
5
3
1

squirrel-in-the-woods mittens

	knit with MC	**V**	knit with MC, duplicate st with CC2	**/**	k2tog with color shown	**R**	M1R with color shown
•	purl with MC	**/**	knit with MC, right half-duplicate st with CC2	****	ssk with color shown	**L**	M1L with color shown
x	knit with CC1	****	knit with MC, left half-duplicate st with CC2				

Mayflooer Mittens

DESIGNED BY ELLI STUBENRAUCH

Fair Isle knitting is a living art and, as the craft moved to other islands in the Shetland group, fresh ideas came into play, including one popular pattern said to be based on linoleum flooring! And so it is with **Elli Stubenrauch's** mittens—she looked no farther than the upholstery of the chair in which she was comfortably slouched while brainstorming ideas for this project. Over the course of a few drafts, the flower motif evolved into more of a third cousin, evolutionarily speaking, but it definitely owes its roots to one *Slipperchairius comfortablus.*

FINISHED SIZE

About 8½" (21.5 cm) circumference and 10¼" (26 cm) long.

YARN

Worsted weight (#4 Medium).

Shown here: Brooklyn Tweed Shelter (100% wool; 140 yd [128 m]/50 g): #21 hayloft (MC; gold), #30 almanac (CC; blue), 1 skein each.

NEEDLES

Cuff: size U.S. 3 (3.25 mm): set of 4 or 5 double-pointed (dpn).

Hand: size U.S. 4 (3.5 mm): set of 4 or 5 dpn.

Adjust needle size if necessary to obtain the correct gauge.

NOTIONS

Marker (m); waste yarn for stitch holders; tapestry needle.

GAUGE

22½ sts and 26½ rnds = 4" (10 cm) in charted patts, worked in rnds on larger needles.

notes

○ This project is deliberately worked at a tighter gauge than is typical for worsted-weight yarn.

○ There are two colors used in every Fair Isle round, so there will always be two strands between the needles to choose from when you work an M1R or M1L increase (see Glossary). Work each increase into the strand that matches the color of the new stitch you are making.

Right Mitten

With CC and smaller needles, CO 40 sts. Arrange sts as evenly as possible on 3 or 4 dpn, place marker (pm), and join for working in rnds, being careful not to twist sts. Rnd begins with the center thumb st.

Cuff

Note: *The unused color should always be stranded across the WS of the work.*

Join MC.

Rnd 1: With MC, knit.

Rnd 2: With MC, *k1, p1; rep from *.

Rnd 3: *K1 MC, p1 MC, k1 CC, p1 MC; rep from *.

Rnd 4: *K1 MC, k3 CC; rep from *.

Rnds 5–15: *K1 MC, p1, CC, k1 CC, p1 CC; rep from *.

Rnd 16: *K1 MC, p1 CC; rep from *.

Rnd 17: K2 MC, *k1 CC, k3 MC; rep from * to last 2 sts, k1 CC, k1 MC.

Rnd 18: With MC, *k1, p1; rep from *—piece measures about 2½" (6.5 cm) from CO.

Next rnd: With MC, *[k1, p1] 2 times, k1f&b (see Glossary), [p1, k1] 2 times, p1f&b (see Glossary); rep from *—48 sts.

Hand

Change to larger needles.

Work Rnds 1–24 of Right Hand chart, being careful not to overlook the central thumb st, and inc as shown on chart (see Notes)—68 sts.

Next rnd: (Rnd 25 of chart) Place first 20 sts onto waste-yarn holder for thumb, work in patt to end—48 sts rem.

Work Rnds 26–51 of chart, dec as shown on chart—20 sts rem after Rnd 51; piece measures about 10¼" (26 cm) from CO.

Cut yarn, leaving a 12" (30.5 cm) tail of CC. Place first 10 sts onto one needle and the last 10 sts onto another needle. Thread CC tail on a tapestry needle and use the Kitchener st (see Glossary) to graft the two 10-st groups tog.

Right Hand

Legend:

☐	MC
☒	CC
╱	k2tog with color shown
╲	ssk with color shown
R	M1R with color shown
L	M1L with color shown

Thumb

Thumb

Return 20 held thumb sts to larger dpn and arrange as evenly as possible on 3 or 4 dpn. Join yarns to beg of thumb sts with RS facing, leaving a 12" (30.5 cm) tail of CC for closing thumb gap later.

Work Rnds 1–8 of Thumb chart, working decs and incs as indicated—16 sts rem.

Next rnd: With CC, *k2tog; rep from *—8 sts rem.

Cut yarn, leaving a 6" (15 cm) tail of CC. Thread CC tail on a tapestry needle, draw through rem sts, pull tight to close hole, and fasten off on WS.

Left Mitten

Cuff

CO and work cuff as for right mitten—48 sts; rnd begins with center thumb st.

Hand

Change to larger needles.

Work Rnds 1–24 of Left Hand chart, being careful not to overlook the central thumb st, and inc as shown on chart—68 sts.

Next rnd: (Rnd 25 of chart) Place first 20 sts onto waste-yarn holder for thumb, work in patt to end—48 sts rem.

Work Rnds 26–51 of chart, dec as shown on chart—20 sts rem after Rnd 51; piece measures about 10¼" (26 cm) from CO.

Close top of hand as for right mitten.

Left Hand

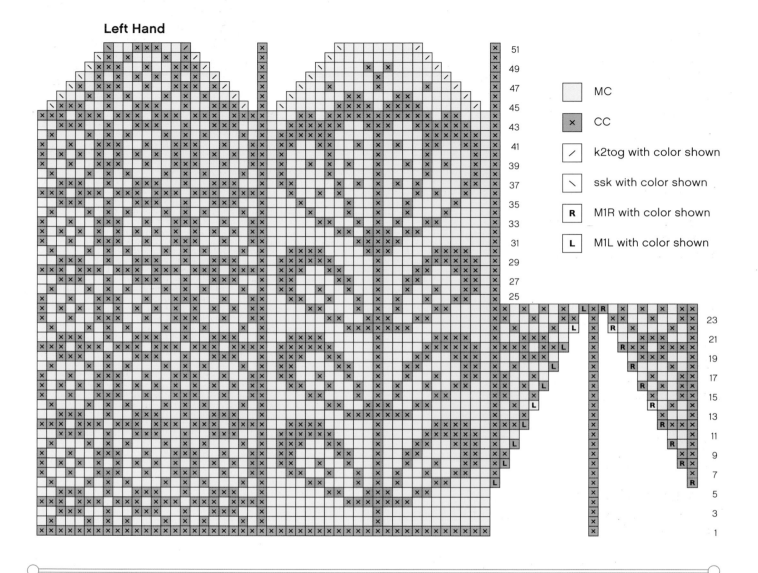

- ☐ MC
- ☒ CC
- ╱ k2tog with color shown
- ╲ ssk with color shown
- R M1R with color shown
- L M1L with color shown

Thumb

Return 20 held thumb sts to larger dpn and arrange as evenly as possible on 3 or 4 dpn. Join yarns to beg of thumb sts with RS facing, leaving a 12" (30.5 cm) tail of CC for closing thumb gap later. Work as for right mitten thumb.

Finishing

Weave in loose ends, using CC tails to close gaps between each thumb and hand.

Block to measurements.

Scandi Sukkalegs

DESIGNED BY
KATE GAGNON OSBORN

Called *sukkalegs* in Shetland dialect, leggings make great take-along projects because they are both small and simple. **Kate Gagnon Osborn** added some Norwegian influence to her two-color leg warmers that feature stacks of partial stars and elegant shaping in vertical stripes. There are a few places where the nonworking yarn is carried for more than an inch (2.5 cm) across the back of the work—you may want to "tack" these floats to the wrong side of the work so they won't catch on your toes as you slip them on.

FINISHED SIZE

About 10" (25.5 cm) lower edge circumference, 12¼" (31 cm) upper edge circumference, and 14¼" (36 cm) long.

YARN

Worsted weight (#4 Medium).

Shown here: The Fibre Company Road to China (65% alpaca, 15% silk, 10% cashmere, 10% camel; 69 yd [63 m]/50 g): moonstone (MC; dark gray-brown) and riverstone (CC; tan), 2 skeins each.

Note: There will be very little MC leftover; you may want to purchase another skein for insurance.

NEEDLES

Ribbing: size U.S. 5 (3.75 mm): set of 5 double-pointed (dpn).

Leg: size U.S. 7 (4.5 mm): set of 5 dpn.

Adjust needle size if necessary to obtain the correct gauge.

NOTIONS

Markers (m); tapestry needle.

GAUGE

21 sts and 22 rnds = 4" (10 cm) in charted patt, worked in rnds on larger needles.

notes

○ Work each M1L or M1R increase into the strand that matches the color of the new stitch you are making.

○ On some chart rounds, you will be required to carry the nonworking color across the back of the work for more than 1" (2.5 cm). In order to reduce the length of the floats while maintaining good tension, "tack" the long floats to the wrong side of the work as described on page 130.

Leg warmer (make 2)

With MC and smaller needles, CO 52 sts. Place marker (pm) and join for working in rnds, being careful not to twist sts. Rnd begins at center back leg.

Rib rnd: *k1, p1; rep from *.

Rep rib rnd until piece measures 1" (2.5 cm) from CO.

Change to larger needles.

Work Rnds 1–65 of Sukkalegs chart, inc as shown—64 sts; piece measures about 12¾" (32.5 cm) from CO.

Change to smaller needles.

With MC, work rib rnd for 1½" (3.8 cm)—piece measures about 14¼" (36 cm) from CO.

Loosely BO all sts in rib patt.

Finishing

Weave in loose ends. Block to measurements.

×	MC	R	M1R with color shown
	CC	L	M1L with color shown
			no stitch

Sukkalegs

52 sts
inc'd to 64 sts

Reeva Hat

DESIGNED BY LISA SHROYER

Seven colors may seem like a lot for a hat, but it's the minimum number of colors **Lisa Shroyer** requires to get the depth and painterly effects she likes in stranded knitting. For this slouchy beret, Lisa chose a wildflower palette of bronze, hot pink, red, blue, white, and shades of brown. Careful color placement within her design creates a shimmer effect, and elegant crown shaping transforms the Moorish patterns of the body into a many-petaled flower! Decorative French knots are added after the knitting is finished, producing an interesting texture and lively focal points.

FINISHED SIZE

About 18¾ (20½, 22)" (47.5 [52, 56] cm) brim circumference and 22 (25, 26½)" (56 [63.5, 67.5] cm) circumference at largest point.

Hat shown measures 22" (56 cm) at brim.

YARN

Sportweight (#2 Fine).

Shown here: Brown Sheep Nature Spun Sport (100% wool; 184 yd [168 m]/50 g): #209 wood moss (MC, dark brown), #104 Grecian olive (A), #N93 latte (B; medium brown), #N46 red fox (C), #105 bougainvillea (D; deep rose), #133 blue fog (E; gray-blue), and #N91 Aran (F; natural), 1 skein each for all sizes.

NEEDLES

Double-knit brim: size U.S. 2 (2.75 mm): 16" (40 cm) circular (cir).

Body: size U.S. 6 (4 mm): 16" (40 cm) cir and set of 5 double-pointed (dpn).

Adjust needle size if necessary to obtain the correct gauge.

NOTIONS

Smooth waste yarn for tubular cast-on; marker (m); tapestry needle.

GAUGE

30 sts and 27 rnds = 4" (10 cm) in Reeva chart patt, worked in rnds on larger needle.

Rnd 2: *Sl 1 pwise with yarn in back (wyb), p1; rep from *.

Rep Rnds 1 and 2 until piece measures 1" (2.5 cm) from CO.

You can remove waste yarn from CO at this point or leave it in place until hat is complete; the CO edge will not ravel.

Body

Inc rnd: *K10 (7, 8), M1 (see Glossary); rep from * to last 0 (24, 0) sts, [k8, M1] 0 (3, 0) times—165 (187, 198) sts.

Change to larger cir needle. Work Rnds 1–16 of Reeva chart 2 times, then work Rnds 17–23 once—150 (170, 180) sts rem after completing Rnd 21.

Note: *As you work the following instructions, change to dpn when necessary.*

Next rnd: Remove m, sl first st pwise wyb, replace m on right needle tip, then work Rnd 24 of chart—120 (136, 144) sts rem.

Work Rnds 25 and 26 of chart.

Next rnd: Remove m, sl first st pwise wyb, replace m on right needle tip; then work Rnd 27 of chart—90 (102, 108) sts rem.

Work Rnds 28–32 of chart—60 (68, 72) sts rem after Rnd 30.

Next rnd: Remove m, sl first st pwise wyb, replace m on right needle tip, then work Rnd 33 of chart—30 (34, 36) sts rem.

Work Rnds 34 and 35 of chart. Cut yarns.

Join MC.

Knit 1 rnd.

Next rnd: *K2tog; rep from *—15 (17, 18) sts rem.

Hat

With waste yarn and smaller cir needle, use the backward-loop method (see Glossary) to CO 75 (82, 88) sts. Do not join.

Brim

Set-up double knitting: With MC, *k1, yo; rep from *—150 (164, 176) sts; do not turn. With RS still facing and making sure not to let the last yo drop from the needle, place marker (pm) and join for working in rnds, being careful not to twist sts.

Work in double knitting as foll:

Rnd 1: *K1, sl 1 with yarn in front (wyf); rep from *.

Knit 1 rnd.

Next rnd: [K2tog] 7 (8, 9) times, k1 (1, 0)—8 (9, 9) sts rem.

Next rnd: [K2tog] 4 times, k0 (1, 1)—4 (5, 5) sts rem.

Work rem sts in rnds for about ½" (1.3 cm) for topknot.

Cut yarn, leaving a 10" (25.5 cm) tail. Thread tail on tapestry needle, draw through rem sts, pull tight to close hole, and fasten off on WS.

Finishing

Weave in loose ends. Soak hat in lukewarm water, squeeze out excess moisture, and block over a dinner plate.

Remove waste yarn from CO if you haven't already done so.

Embroidery

With F threaded on a tapestry needle, work French knots (see Glossary) as shown on chart: between 2 color B sts in Rnd 9 and directly on top of the center color B st in Rnd 25.

Reeva

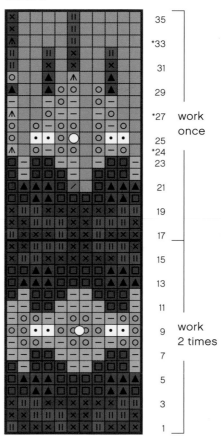

35
*33
31
29
*27   work once
25
*24
23
21
19
17
15
13
11
9   work 2 times
7
5
3
1

11-st repeat
dec'd to 2-st repeat

*See instructions.

□ MC		• F	
‖ A		╱ k2tog with color shown	
○ B		ʌ sl 2, k1 p2sso with color shown	
✕ C		◯ knit with color shown, French knot with F	
▲ D			no stitch
– E		□ pattern repeat	

Design Notebook

> There are never more than two colors
> in a single row of Fair Isle knitting.

Happily, Fair Isle knitting is not as complicated as it may seem. But if you've never done it before, you will want to set aside some uninterrupted time so you can concentrate. There are several things you'll need to learn all at once, so don't be discouraged if you don't immediately master them all.

Fair Isle knitting is a particular type of stranded knitting in which two colors are worked in the same row according to a charted pattern. Though the colors may change from row to row, there is always a dominant "pattern" color and a less dominant "background color." The pattern motifs themselves are most typically symmetrical, both vertically and horizontally. Within each row of knitting, the color not in use is stranded along the reverse (wrong) side of the work to form "floats." In general, there are few stitches between color changes so that the floats are relatively short. These are the building blocks for great designs, no matter what type of project you'd like to knit.

To start, you'll need to know how to hold two colors of yarn at the same time. Knitting with two colors takes practice, but, fortunately, most of the patterns in this book are knitted in the round in the traditional Fair Isle way so you only have to master knitting with two colors, not purling. It's much easier to work in rounds because you are always looking at the right side of the work, and you can see the pattern motifs emerge row by row. Only three projects—the Babsie Bird (page 68), Mud Cloth Bag (page 94), and the pockets of the Bressay Dress (page 48)—involve working back and forth in rows. For these projects, you'll need to purl with two colors, and you'll have to read the charts in the opposite direction on wrong-side rows. But all three projects require just small bits of knitting this way and are well worth the extra effort.

You'll also want to make informed decisions about the types of yarn that are best suited for Fair Isle knitting, because not all yarns are created equal when it comes to stranded colorwork. And because Fair Isle knitting is all about color, you'll want to understand a little about color theory, so that choosing colors will be fun instead of intimidating.

Finally, you'll want to take proper care in finishing to make your project perfect. Shetlanders take their finishing very seriously and so should you! Find out why wet-blocking is so crucial for stranded colorwork.

Knitting in the Fair Isle Tradition
Holding the Yarn

To keep your yarns from tangling, place one ball on each side of your body.

In traditional Fair Isle patterns, there are only two colors in any row of knitting. For speed, you'll want to hold the two colors simultaneously so that you can switch from one to the other without dropping the old color to pick up and tension the new. Though it will likely feel awkward at first, just remember that you learned to knit with one yarn and, with similar practice, you can learn to knit with two. You can choose to hold both yarns in your right hand or your left hand, or you can hold one in each hand. Try out the methods described in the box on page 129 to see which method is most comfortable for you—no one way is better than another. If you find it hard to learn from text and illustrations, join a knitting group or take a class at your local yarn shop—often just watching someone knitting with two yarns will make the actions click from your head to your hands. And remember, practice makes perfect!

YARN DOMINANCE

For an even appearance on the right side of the work, it is important to hold and manipulate the pattern and background yarn in a consistent manner. For most knitters, the yarn that is held the farthest to the left (no matter how you hold the yarn) will appear the most dominant in the colorwork pattern. This position causes the float to strand lower, or lie beneath the floats of the yarn held to the right. In Fair Isle knitting, the pattern color should be most dominant. Therefore, always hold the pattern color to the left and the background color to the right. There are slight differences in individual technique and not everyone will have the same results; it may be a while before you can tell which of your yarns is dominant. The most important thing to remember is to be consistent in how you hold the yarns.

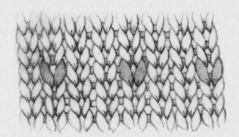

The yarn that comes from beneath the other will make a slightly larger stitch that will be somewhat more prominent.

Holding Both Yarns in the Right Hand

Hold both yarns in your right hand so that the background color (light) is tensioned over your index finger and the pattern color (dark) is tensioned over your middle finger. Manipulate your index finger to work the background color; turn your hand slightly to manipulate the pattern color from your middle finger.

Holding Both Yarns in the Left Hand

Hold both yarns in your left hand with both strands over your left index finger and so that the pattern color (dark) is to the left of the background color (light). "Pick" the necessary color with each stitch.

Holding One Yarn in Each Hand

Hold the background color (light) in your right hand with the yarn tensioned over your right index finger. Hold the pattern color (dark) in your left hand with the yarn tensioned over your left index finger. Knit the background color by moving it into place with your right index finger; knit the pattern color by "picking" it from your left index finger.

  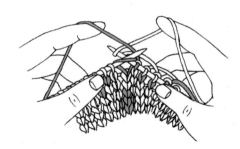

Floats

> The floats along the back should span the width of the knitted stitches without stretching or sagging.

In two-color knitting, the color not in use is carried loosely—or stranded—across the wrong side of the work to create "floats." The background yarn floats behind the work when stitches are worked in the pattern color and vice versa. Simply knit with the desired yarn, allowing the other to strand across the back. Be sure to keep the new stitches spread out along the right-hand needle to ensure that the yarn not in use will strand across the true width of the just-knitted stitches. If the floats are too short, puckers will appear in the fabric. If the floats are too long, the stitches can become loose and appear too tall in comparison. In either case, the knitted fabric will look sloppy and uneven.

In traditional Fair Isle knitting, floats are rarely longer than 1" (2.5 cm), and traditional Shetland wool is quite "sticky," which makes even longer floats inconsequential. However, in other stranded traditions—Scandinavian, for example—extra-long floats can be quite common and care should be taken to trap them with the working yarn.

If such long floats are stacked one on top of another over a series of rows (or rounds), take care to stagger the catch points so that you don't inadvertently cause a visible vertical line along the right side of the knitting. Some knitters like to catch floats often—every third or even every stitch—to effectively eliminate the floats altogether. Doing so will make a denser and less flexible fabric that is more similar to a woven fabric, and that will affect the overall gauge. Be sure to measure your gauge from a generous swatch in which you've caught the floats in the same manner you plan to catch them in your project.

Preventing Long Floats

To prevent long floats that can catch on fingers and distort the stitches, floats should be no longer than 1" (2.5 cm) long. If a float needs to span a wider distance, it's best to trap or "catch" it with the working yarn to keep it snug against the back of the work.

To trap a long float against the back of the fabric, insert the right needle tip into the next stitch on the left-hand needle, place the nonworking yarn over the right needle (**Figure 1; nonworking yarn is dark**), knit the stitch with the working yarn as usual, then lower the nonworking yarn (**Figure 2**) and knit the following stitch as usual.

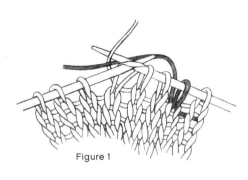

Figure 1

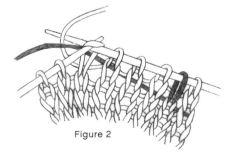

Figure 2

The floats should strand evenly and consistently across the wrong side of the work. When worked consistently, they will form a pleasing pattern of their own.

Yarn Choice

Traditional Fair Isle knitting is worked in wool from the hardy Shetland breed of sheep that is native to the Shetland Islands. Shetland wool is very soft but has a tight crimp that gives the yarn "tooth" and makes it a bit "sticky." This type of yarn is ideal for stranded knitting because the floats tend to grab onto the knitted fabric, and the knitting is slow to ravel when steeks are cut (see page 136). Additionally, Shetland wool occurs in a wide variety of natural colors, at least nine of which are distinct enough to be assigned names. This allows for richly patterned garments made entirely from undyed yarn! The Valenzi Cardigan (page 76), with its range of natural hues, gives a nod to this traditional look. Shetland wool takes dyes beautifully as well and is available in seemingly unlimited colors—one company produces more than 165 colors! Babsie Bird (page 68), Morroless Socks (page 20), Mirry-Dancers Yoked Pullover (page 26), and Mirknin Hat and Scarf (page 44) all are knitted from traditional Shetland yarns from Shetland.

In addition to Shetland, there are other wools that are suitable for stranded knitting—try a variety to learn which you like best. Many new yarn companies have sprung up in the past few years that make use of local wool. Green Mountain Spinnery's Wonderfully Woolly, used in Squirrel-in-the-Woods Mittens (page 106), is made from wool from local Vermont sheep. For her Lumesadu Gloves (page 12), Nancy Bush used yarn from Elemental Affects, a company that uses wool from 100 percent purebred Shetland sheep born and raised in Montana. Brooklyn Tweed's yarns Shelter, used for the elegant Mayflooer Mittens (page 112) and Loft used for the Bressay Dress (page 48), Quince and Co.'s Chickadee, used for the Peerie Weerie Booties (page 58), and St-Denis Nordique, used for Kat Coyle's luminous Ketlin Skirt (page 34), all use wool carefully sourced from small producers in North America.

Adding Colors

Although you can use a single color for the pattern and a single color for the background for an entire project, as in Kate Gagnon Osborn's Scandi Sukkalegs (page 118), Fair Isle patterns evolve into beautiful mosaics when bands of pattern colors are worked against bands of background colors as in Elinor Brown's remarkable Mirknin Hat and Scarf (page 44) and Kat Coyle's cheery Ketlin Skirt (page 34). When you want to change a pattern or background color, simply cut the old yarn, leaving a 4" to 6" (10 to 15 cm) tail, then start knitting with the new color, also leaving a 4" to 6" (10 to 15 cm) tail (you'll weave in the ends later). If the color will be used again in two or three rounds, you can simply let it fall to the back of the work and pick it up again when it's needed. I did this in the center of the motifs in both the Morroless Socks (page 20) and Valenzi Cardigan (page 76). If the color won't be used for more than three rounds, it's best to cut and rejoin the yarn to prevent puckers forming from long vertical floats (and to prevent the multiple balls of yarn tangling on each other).

Of course, you may use other yarns. But you'll have the best results if the yarn is prepared from fibers that have been processed the same as Shetland yarn; that is, fibers that have been carded, not combed. Yarns spun from combed fibers are smooth and can be less forgiving of uneven stitches, but they are by no means unsuitable for Fair Isle knitting. There are many lovely yarns and blends available in beautiful colors. Just be aware that it might take a little extra effort to get the same result that you'd get from a "sticky" yarn. In fact, these yarns are often worth the extra bit of effort required—who could pass up a chance to use Road to China, a luxurious blend of alpaca, silk, cashmere, and camel, featured in Kate Gagnon Osborn's Scandi Sukkalegs (page 118)? And who isn't tempted to try a wool blend that includes nettles, as in the Classic Elite Woodland used for Mags Kandis's Mud Cloth Bag (page 94)? It can be very exciting to step beyond tradition.

It is wise to give a thought to yarn weight. Traditional garments in Shetland are made in two-ply jumper-weight wool, a kind of heavy fingering-weight yarn. I used this traditional wool in the Morroless Socks (page 20), and it is perfect for the scale of Babsie Bird (page 68) as well. Though not strictly traditional, the lovely Sunday Knits yarns used in SpillyJane's Mushroom Kelliemuffs (page 40) closely approximates this same weight.

Other weights of yarn can be suitable as well. Ysolda Teague used a fine laceweight yarn worked at a loose gauge for her Kulli Cowl (page 8), in which she pairs gossamer garter stitch with very textural Fair Isle sections for an interesting and creative use of materials. Kat Coyle's Ketlin Skirt (page 34) is knitted with St-Denis Nordique, a DK-weight yarn that provides the perfect weight and drape for a swingy skirt. The solid worsted-weight yarn used in the Valenzi Cardigan (page 76) produces a cozy sweater that is thick without annoying bulk. Finally, Kirsten Kapur's Hap-Lapghan (page 62) is knitted in a lofty and light bulky-weight yarn that is also springy and stretchy, resulting in a comforting cover against the chill.

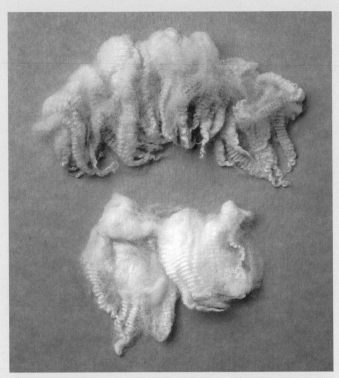

Shetland wool has a tight crimp. Top: Unwashed locks. Bottom: Washed locks.

The same or similar pattern can look quite different, depending on the yarn choice. Left: Traditional Shetland two-ply jumper-weight yarn (Jamieson & Smith and Jamieson wool). Center: Smooth DK-weight yarn (St-Denis Nordique). Right: Traditional bulky-weight Icelandic wool (Alafoss Lopi).

Reading Charts

To keep track of large motifs,
place a stitch marker on your needle
after every pattern repeat.

To help keep track of the pattern when
using double-pointed needles, orient
the stitches so that each
needle begins with the first stitch
of a repeat and ends with the
last stitch of a repeat.

Most Fair Isle patterns are presented in a charted format that represents what the knitted fabric will look like when viewed from the right side. Each square in a chart represents a single stitch, and the color of each square (and the symbol within it) indicates the color to use for that particular stitch. Most charts represent a full pattern repeat both widthwise and lengthwise, with balancing stitches when necessary. Stitches that are to be repeated across a row or round of knitting are outlined in a red "pattern repeat" box.

Chart rows are read from the bottom to the top, right-side (odd-numbered) rows are read from right to left, and wrong-side (even-numbered) rows are read from left to right. When working in rounds, as for most traditional Fair Isle knitting, every round is considered a right-side row, and every row of the chart is read from right to left. The Morroless Socks (page 20) is one of the projects that was knitted in rounds, in which case each row of the chart was read from right to left. When knitting back and forth in rows, however, the wrong-side rows are read from left to right, and the stitches are purled to maintain

Morroless

16-st repeat
work 4 times

 MC   C   F

 A   D   G

 B   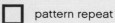 E   pattern repeat

stockinette stitch. In Gudrun Johnston's Bressay Dress (page 48) both methods are used. The yoke is knitted circularly in rounds, while the charming pockets are knitted flat in rows (their small size making the knitting manageable). Mags Kandis has always preferred knitting colorwork flat and in pieces, which is how she worked her Mud Cloth Bag (page 94). She kept things simple by limiting the design to just two colors.

There are many books that offer collections of Fair Isle patterns in chart format—some of these great resources are listed in the bibliography on page 157. Traditionally, these charts were printed in black and white—the pattern stitches are represented by black dots (originally made by a wooden matchstick dipped in ink); the background stitches are represented by blank squares. This is a convenient way to chart and get a sense for the overall pattern—you can always add the colors of your choice in colored pencil.

Keep in mind that circular knitting grows in a spiral so that the pattern actually swirls around the circular tube like the stripes of a candy cane. You may suddenly think you've "gone off pattern," but chances are that you have just reached the beginning of a new round. At this point, there will be a break in the pattern—the end of one round doesn't match up perfectly with the beginning of the next round. This also means that there is a slight jog in the colorwork pattern at the boundary between two rounds, something that happens in all circular colorwork knitting. But don't worry—you can camouflage the jog by following the instructions in the sidebar at right or simply by weaving in the ends carefully, as explained in detail on page 144.

Jogless Join

To hide the jog that occurs between the last stitch of one round and the first stitch of the second, especially when working single-color stripes, try Meg Swansen's jogless join.

Work to the end of the round with the new color. At the start of the next round, insert the needle tip from back to front into the stitch in the row below the first stitch of the round **(Figure 1)**, lift this stitch up and place it onto the tip of the left needle, in front of the stitch that's already there **(Figure 2)**. Then knit these two stitches (one each of the old and new color) together to bring the height of the first stitch even with the height of the last stitch of the round.

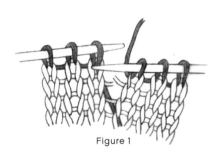

Figure 1

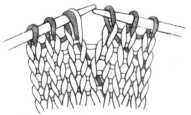

Figure 2

The Importance of Gauge

The first step in any knitting project, whether you plan to follow an existing pattern or design one of your own, is to knit a generous swatch to determine the gauge. Be sure to knit your gauge swatch the same as you plan to knit your project—in rounds if you plan to work circularly; in rows if you plan to work flat.

The gauge is the number of stitches and rows or rounds in an inch of knitting that you'll get with the yarn and needles that you plan to use for your project. Where gauge swatches are concerned, the bigger, the better. You can get a better approximation of the gauge that you'll get when knitting a large piece, such as a sweater, if your gauge swatch measures at least 6" (15 cm) in both width and length. Smaller swatches don't give you time to settle into the rhythm of the knitting before you come to the end of a row or round. It is crucial to match the reported gauge in a pattern to end up with the specified finished dimensions and a proper fit. If you get more or fewer stitches per inch than specified in a pattern, your garment will be either too small or too big.

If you plan to design a garment for yourself, the gauge swatch will help you determine the thickness and hand, or drape, of the finished fabric. If the fabric feels too loose, try again with smaller needles; conversely, if the fabric feels too stiff, try again with larger needles. Keep adjusting needle size until you're satisfied with the fabric.

It's not uncommon for knitters to experience a slightly looser gauge in bands of solid color worked between Fair Isle patterns. If you find this happens, try working the solid-color bands on needles one size smaller. Often, the floats along the back of the work cause the stitches to be a bit tighter in Fair Isle sections than in stockinette sections worked in a single color.

Fair Isle Gauge-Swatch Tips

○ Knit the swatch using the Fair Isle pattern(s) you plan to use in your garment. Different pattern motifs can work up to different gauges, based on the number and length of the floats. Ideally, you'll want to cast on enough stitches to work two or more repeats of the pattern so you'll see how the motifs appear side by side and one on top of another.

○ Include all of the colors you plan to use in your project in the swatch. Don't be tempted to knit the swatch with a single pattern and a single background color if there will be multiple colors in the project. Yarn diameter can vary between light and dark natural colors and between natural colors and dyed colors. While these differences may be small, they can affect the gauge over a large number of stitches.

○ Use the method of knitting that you plan to use in the garment—if the garment will be knitted in the round, knit the gauge swatch in the round as well. Many knitters knit and purl at different gauges, and a piece worked in rows (which alternates rows of knit stitches with rows of purl stitches) will not measure the same as one worked in rounds (in which all of the stitches are knitted all of the time).

○ Before measuring the gauge, finish the swatch the same way you plan to finish your project.

Once you are happy with the look and feel of your gauge swatch, finish it—most likely by wet-blocking—as you plan to finish the garment. Allow it to dry thoroughly, then lay the swatch on a flat surface (if you knitted the swatch in the round, cut the tube open so it will lie flat) and use a ruler to measure the number of stitches in 4" (10 cm) in width and the number of rows/rounds in 4" (10 cm) in length. Most patterns specify gauge over 4" (10 cm), but if you need to know the number of stitches or rows/rounds per 1" (2.5 cm), divide the number of stitches and rows/rounds by 4.

Steeks

Steeks are "extra" stitches that allow garments that are knitted in rounds to be cut open along the center front, neck, and armholes. Although many knitters shy away from cutting their work, it's much easier to knit a circular tube without interruption and then cut open and finish steeks than it is to work a Fair Isle cardigan back and forth in rows. Many of the projects in this book are designed as tubes that are knitted in rounds, such as Kat Coyle's Ketlin Skirt (page 34), Carrie Bostick Hoge's Peerie Weerie Booties (page 58), and Lisa Shroyer's Reeva Hat (page 122). But sweaters need openings for heads and arms and, in the case of the Valenzi Cardigan (page 76), an opening along the center front. By adding steek stitches, you can knit the entire body (and both sleeves) in rounds, which makes it easier to follow charted patterns. During the finishing process, the extra stitches are reinforced and then sharp scissors are used to cut the knitted fabric between the reinforcements to create the openings.

Steeks can be as narrow as three stitches or as wide as twelve stitches. Generally, narrower steeks are worked on sticky wool, whereas wider steeks are favored for more slippery yarns. When working cardigans from the bottom up, steek stitches are typically included in the original cast-on or just after the lower ribbing or edging is worked

(as for the Valenzi Cardigan on page 76). For armhole and neck openings, steek stitches are typically added after the initial row of bind-off used to shape these openings.

Steek stitches are typically worked in a striped pattern that alternates one stitch each of the background and pattern colors. If there is an even number of steek stitches, the outermost stitches are worked in the background color, the center two stitches are worked in the pattern color, and the others alternate between the two. Stitches for the frontband, neckband, or sleeves are picked up along the outermost background-color stitches, and the steek is cut between the center two pattern-color stitches. If there is an odd number of steek stitches, the outermost stitches are worked in the background color, and the other stitches alternate between the pattern and background; the steek is cut along the center pattern-color stitch. For patterns that include the traditional "peak," or diamond-shape, patterns, such as in the Valenzi Cardigan, it is useful to designate the stitches as either "dark" or "light," choosing the one that is closest to the main color as the background color. For this sweater, the main color was

Reinforcing Steeks

WITH HAND OR MACHINE STAYSTITCHES

To secure the knitting, sew a line of contrasting straight stitches down the middle of each stitch that borders the center two steek stitches (dashed lines in **Figure 1**). Note that the center steek stitches are both the same color. You can work by hand with sturdy sewing thread in a circular motion of backstitches, or you can sew small straight stitches by machine. With sharp scissors, carefully cut between the center two stitches.

Gently turn the cut edges to the wrong side of the garment, tacking into place if desired.

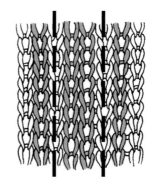

Figure 1

WITH SLIP-STITCH CROCHET

With contrasting yarn and working from right to left, *insert the crochet hook through the back leg (shown dark) of the stitch closest to the two center steek stitches, then through the front leg (shown light) of the closest center steek stitch **(Figure 2)**, wrap the yarn around the hook, then pull this new loop through all loops on the hook.

Repeat from * for every stitch.

When you reach the neck edge, cut the yarn and secure the last stitch. Turn the work 180 degrees, so that the other side of the steek is closest to you, and repeat the process. With sharp scissors, carefully cut between the center two stitches.

The cut edges will naturally roll to the wrong side along the crocheted stitches; tack them in place if desired.

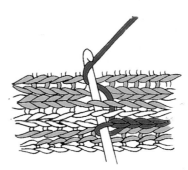

Figure 2

oatmeal, so the lightest color was always designated as the background color.

If you use a traditional Shetland wool yarn that sticks to itself and resists raveling, it is possible to cut the steeks without any additional reinforcement of the stitches. If you are fearful that your knitting might ravel or if you used a somewhat slippery yarn, reinforce the steek stitches with hand or machine staystitches or slip-stitch crochet before you cut, as described in the sidebar above.

Designing in Fair Isle

Designing your own Fair Isle garment can be a lot of fun. Start your happy pursuits with something simple, a cowl or the lower edge of a skirt, for example, then follow these simple guidelines. Before you know it, you'll be ready to tackle more complex patterns!

Pattern Choice

Venture beyond tradition and invent your own motifs.

Traditional Fair Isle patterns never have more than two colors in a given row, and the colors change frequently so that there are rarely more than seven or eight consecutive stitches of the same color. This ensures that the floats on the reverse side of the work are never too long. The occasional times when longer floats are necessary are limited to just one or two rows within the full pattern motif. Fortunately, most traditional motifs are symmetrical in both vertical and horizontal directions, and oftentimes across the diagonal as well. This makes it easy to memorize the motifs as you knit—when you reach the midpoint, you simply have to work the pattern in reverse to the other edge.

Typical pattern motifs fall into several basic categories. Peerie patterns, which mean "small" in Shetland dialect, are narrow patterns that range from two to seven rows. For her Peerie Weerie Booties (page 58), Carrie Bostick Hoge chose to repeat a single staggered peerie pattern in different colors. Gudrun Johnston decorated the yoke, hem, and pockets of her playful Bressay Dress (page 48) with an assortment of peerie patterns. Both Courtney

Kelley (Fara Raglan; page 84) and Ysolda Teague (Kulli Cowl; page 8) chose to separate a series of peerie patterns with solid-color stripes for very attractive, yet very different, results.

Border patterns are larger and typically span between eight and fifteen rows. The most classic form is an OXO motif made up of lozenge shapes that alternate with X shapes. Elinor Brown chose this type of border pattern for her Mirknin Hat and Scarf (page 44). The star motif (borrowed from Norway) is another familiar border pattern that is used in combination with a small peerie in the Morroless Socks (page 20). Kate Gagnon Osborn stacked elements of a star to create an entirely different motif in her Scandi Sukkalegs (page 118). Nancy Bush chose to include both a border and peerie pattern to adorn her Lumesadu Gloves (page 12).

Another traditional motif is a diamond shape called "peaks," which provides a means to shade colors from light to dark, then back to light. The Valenzi Cardigan (page 76) is a good example of this progression from light to dark, or dark to light, and then back again, which is an important characteristic of many Fair Isle patterns.

Adhering to tradition will help to get you started designing your own garments, but don't be limited by convention. Venture beyond the traditional and invent your own motifs, as Elli Stubenrauch did for her Squirrel-in-the-Woods Mittens (page 106). Look at your surroundings for inspiration—in the old days, Shetland knitters were inspired by such mundane things as the patterns in their linoleum floors. For her Mayflooer Mittens (page 112), Elli copied the fabric in her knitting chair! Pare down a pattern into its most graphic element, as in Cheryl Burke's Mirry-Dancers Yoked Pullover (page 26) and Kirsten Kapur's very modern Hap-Lapghan (page 62). Turn the whole idea on its head and pop a traditional border pattern into a unique construction, as Norah Gaughan did for her Mareel Shrug (page 98).

A Tiny Bit of Color Theory

Although color theory was developed for mixing paint in fine-art painting, it provides a vocabulary to use when describing color.

Hue is simply another name for color, as in red, blue, or yellow. Two different blues might be described as being close in hue, while yellow or red are different hues. The twelve-part color wheel designates red, yellow, and blue hues as the three primary colors. In theory, these are the foundation of all other colors. Mix two primary colors in equal amounts to produce the three secondary colors—red plus yellow produces orange, yellow plus blue produces green, and blue plus red produces violet. The six tertiary colors have different percentages of the two primaries. For example, a mixture of more yellow than blue will produce yellow-green; a mixture of more blue than yellow will produce blue-green.

For our purposes, the color wheel is useful for understanding color relationships. Colors that are positioned next to one another on the wheel are called **analogous colors.** Analogous colors are almost always harmonious when used together. **Complementary colors,** such as blue and orange, lie across from each other on the color wheel. When used together, they will appear vibrant and provide high contrast. Lucinda Guy used this contrast for her playful Babsie Bird (page 68).

Split-complementary colors are derived from the two colors adjacent to a color's complement. For example, red and orange are split-complements of blue-green. Split-complementary colors often make a pleasing arrangement. Lisa Shroyer used this concept when choosing colors for her Reeva Hat (page 122). She used several shades of red that progress to a pale blue, which is one of their split-complements. The result is a shimmer effect against the range of neutral colors in the background. Split-complementary colors also prove pleasing to the eye in Kat Coyle's Ketlin Skirt (page 34).

Keep in mind that the color wheel only describes hues. Tint, tone,

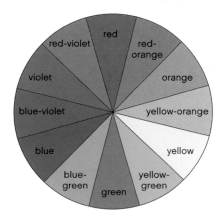

shade, and value are responsible for the great variations in color. A **tint** is made by adding white to a hue—pink is a tint made from combining red and white. A **tone** is made by adding gray and a **shade** is made by adding black. In terms of yarn, it might be more helpful to think in terms of adding different colors of fleece. For example, if black fleece is added to a brightly dyed red one, a darker shade of red will be produced. If white fleece is added to the same dyed red fleece, a lighter pinkish color will be produced.

When it comes to Fair Isle knitting, the most important feature is color value, which is a measure of the color's relative lightness or darkness. There needs to be sufficient contrast between the pattern and background colors for the motifs to stand out. In addition, most traditional patterns involve symmetry—the colors are arranged in value sequences that are symmetrical about a center point. The most pleasing Fair Isle patterns involve a play of colors of different values that change symmetrically.

Play around with the placement of the motifs. Elinor Brown stacked the OXO patterns in her Mirknin Hat and Scarf (page 44), whereas similar motifs are staggered in my Valenzi Cardigan (page 76) and Carrie Bostick Hoge's Peerie Weerie Booties (page 58). For variety, try interconnecting a motif to create an allover pattern, as Mags Kandis did for her Mud Cloth Bag (page 94).

Color Choice

Choosing colors is half the fun of Fair Isle knitting. Although there are never more than two colors in any row or round, stunning color effects are possible, from relatively simple stripes, as in Cheryl Burke's Mirry-Dancers Yoked Pullover (page 26), to visually rich mosaics, as in Elinor Brown's Mirknin Hat and Scarf (page 44).

The designers have taken the worry out of selecting color for the projects in this book, but it's helpful to understand a bit about color theory and follow some guidelines when making substitutions or designing on your own. Keep in mind that it's important to have access to clear natural daylight when choosing colors so that you'll see the true colors. Evening or dim or artificial light can obscure true colors and minimize the differences between close colors. You don't want to be surprised by colors that look significantly different in daylight, as I was by the swatches shown below.

These swatches are nearly the same, but the one on the left was worked at night under dim artificial light. It wasn't until the next morning that it became evident that the purple used for the center of the OXO motif was different.

COMBINING COLORS

Use variegated yarn to give the appearance of complexity without the fuss of changing yarns.

To apply color theory to your yarn choice, gather a group of colors that you like (they can be from divergent color groups), then separate the light and dark colors into separate piles (**Photo 1**). Weed out any supersaturated colors, such as vibrant red or electric blue, and set them aside in a third pile. Until you've had a lot of practice, such colors are best left for occasional accents. Add any odd colors to this third pile, as well as colors that you might not like much. You'd be surprised how a bit of something you don't care for can add just the right zing to a Fair Isle pattern.

Fine-tune the arrangement of colors in each group by arranging the yarns in a sequence of value from dark to light (**Photo 2**). This can be tricky, and there will be times that you'll have trouble deciding where some colors fit into the sequence (see the different sequence of the light colors in **Photo 2** and **Photo 3**), but it is a very good exercise in color and value and will help you recognize subtle differences. On the other hand, there are hours of enjoyment to be had—you can make any number of pleasing arrangements by simply rearranging the same group of colors.

Kat Coyle played with the sequences in her Ketlin Skirt (page 34). She used the same arrangement of pattern motif colors in the border pattern, while she used wider bands of turquoise and pale yellow for the background in the bottom motif and single rows of neutrals in the top border. Likewise, she kept the cat heads black but changed the arrangement of background colors in the two pattern bands.

Photo 1. Arrange your yarn in three piles—one of light colors (right), one of dark colors (left), and one of supersaturated and odd colors (top).

Photo 2. Arrange the colors in value sequences from light to dark.

Photo 3. Choose a sequence of three light colors and a sequence of three dark colors.

Photo 4. Make a black-and-white photocopy of the two sequences to ensure there is enough contrast between the two groups.

Photo 5. Wrap the colors around card stock to get a better idea how the colors appear next to one another.

Next, choose three colors from each of the light and dark groups (the colors do not need to be the same hue, just from the same group) and place them side by side **(Photo 3)**. To ensure there will be enough contrast between the two groups, the lightest dark color should be darker than the darkest light color. If you're unsure that there will be enough contrast, make a black-and-white photocopy **(Photo 4)** or scan of the yarn (wrap each group of yarns around a piece of card stock as in **Photo 5** to make this easier) to focus on the value differences. If you can see contrast between the colors in the photocopy or scan, there will likely be enough contrast when they are knitted up. If you're in doubt, twist a length of the two colors together (**Photo 6**). There will be enough contrast if you can see two distinct colors (as for a marled yarn), but if the two blend visually into a single color, they will do the same in the knitted fabric and the pattern will not appear distinct from the background. Keep in mind that while two colors may not have sufficient value contrast to work one as a pattern color and the other as a background color, they may be very successful if both are used in the same group—either pattern or background.

Finally, add one or two of those wacky colors that you set aside at the beginning for the very center row of a pattern motif. Chances are that a "wild" color will bring an unexpected touch of excitement and zing to your other color choices (**Photos 7 and 8**). Sometimes, colors you don't particularly like can become magically beautiful when strategically placed in a sequence of other colors. There's no end to the fun you can have experimenting with color!

Need more inspiration? Look at the world around you—nature is ablaze with color combinations that will translate beautifully to Fair Isle patterns. Look for color combinations everywhere from the landscape against the horizon to the label on a package in the supermarket. Keep in mind that colors change by the hour, and the colors you see in the bright morning light can be significantly different from the colors you see in the late afternoon. Train your eyes to see color relationships wherever you go and you'll soon find you have many more color combinations than you have time to explore.

COLOR PLACEMENT

One of the most remarkable features of color is that a particular color can appear different, depending on the surrounding color(s), as shown in **Photos 9 and 10.** The three swatches in **Photo 9** are all knitted in the same OXO pattern with the same colors. The sample on the left is worked with dark pattern colors against light background colors. In this case, the dark pattern colors shade from

Photo 6. Although these two yarns appear to be sufficiently different, they blend into a single color when twisted around each other, indicating that there is too little value difference for them to work successfully as pattern and background.

Photo 7. Although these four colors make a nice palette, the overall effect is a bit dull.

Photo 8. Add one or two lively colors for more visual excitement.

Photo 9. You can get entirely different looks, depending on how the same colors are arranged.

Photo 10. The same pattern can look completely different, depending on the colors used. Left: Navy, periwinkle,and burgundy pattern colors against a light gray background. Right: A solid black pattern against a background that changes from turquoise to red and yellow.

light to dark, then back to light. For the sample in the center, dark colors are used for the background, and the light pattern colors shade from light to dark. The lower OXO band in the sample on the right is worked with both light pattern colors that shade from dark to light against a dark background. The upper band is worked with dark pattern colors that shade from dark to light against a light background.

For the Valenzi Cardigan (page 76), I began with a series of dark colors against a solid light background. I then reversed the sequence at the center of the garment and worked a series of light pattern colors against a dark solid background color. For the Morroless Socks (page 20), I combined three supersaturated colors of three very different hues for the background and tamed them with nearly neutral pattern colors.

SWATCHING

If you want to try your hand at choosing your own colorways, begin by swatching some small peerie patterns. Not only will you get practice stranding colors, you'll have the opportunity to try a number of color combinations over relatively few rounds or rows of knitting, as shown in **Photo 11**. Any of the motifs in Ysolda Teague's

Kulli Cowl (page 8) make a good springboard for simple two-color motifs. Just by reversing the colors—work the pattern in the background color and the background in the pattern color—you can get an entirely different look. Next, try substituting a different color for both the pattern and background, maintaining the same degree of contrast—a different color that's as dark as the red and another color that's as light as the gray. Follow up with a larger border pattern that consists of nine to eleven rows or rounds, such as the star motif Nancy Bush used in her Lumesadu Gloves (page 12), and introduce more colors for the pattern or background.

For more complicated-looking results, try a variety of shades for the pattern or background color. For example, in the Valenzi Cardigan on page 76 a dark border pattern shades from light to dark, then back to light, while the white background color remains the same. Later the same pattern is worked against a dark background, still changing from light to dark and back to light again. Try the complete opposite—keep the pattern color constant while shading the background from light to dark, then back to light. What happens if you change the shading from light to dark to light? You'll be surprised by how much you can alter the look of a Fair Isle motif by simply changing where the colors appear in the pattern.

design notebook

For a sophisticated look, shade both the pattern and background colors. Shade both from light to dark and back again, or vice versa. Or shade one set from dark to light and the other from light to dark, making sure there is enough contrast between each pattern/background pairing for the pattern motifs to read clearly. Elinor Brown shaded both the pattern and background colors from dark to light in her Mirknin Hat and Scarf (page 44). But to keep things interesting, she used a bright red for the center of the motif. This bold spot of color adds life without disrupting the overall pattern.

You may find that swatching is so much fun that you find yourself wanting to try "just one more" color combination before making a final decision. Save your swatches as so many trophies. If you label them with the yarns, needles, motifs, and color placement used, you'll have a permanent record for future inspiration. Or, turn the larger swatches into pillows or combine the smaller ones into an afghan, for example.

Photo 11. The same shade of purplish gray appears to change color and even disappear, depending on the color it is paired with.

Finishing

Weaving in Ends

One of the downsides to knitting with multiple colors is that there will be multiple ends to weave in. While this can seem daunting if left to the end, it's not at all onerous if you keep up with it as you go. Many Shetland knitters don't bother weaving in the tails—they simply knot the ends and let them hang on the wrong side of the garment.

To weave in the ends with a tapestry needle, leave a 4" to 6" (10 to 15 cm) tail of yarn hanging from the wrong side of the work whenever you change colors. Take a break every few rows or rounds, thread the tail on a tapestry needle, and run the point of the needle along the wrong side, following the direction the yarn would have been coming from—to the right for the beginning tail of a new color; to the left for the ending tail of an old color. Catch the tail through the back of eight to ten stitches, working into stitches of the same color whenever possible. Weave in the ends as if the pattern were worked in concentric circles (instead of the spiral it truly forms) to help close gaps at color changes. Blocking will obscure slight imperfections.

Correcting Mistakes

Take time to examine your work closely as you go to prevent errors. But even the most careful knitter will sometimes make mistakes. Simple mistakes that involve just a stitch or two in the wrong color can be corrected by working duplicate stitches (see Glossary) in the correct color. More serious errors that disrupt the pattern over larger areas will require ripping out. If the error is only a row or two below the needles, you may want to "unknit" stitch by stitch. If the error is several rows below, it is most efficient to take the piece off the needles, rip out to before the mistake, then carefully return the stitches onto the needles.

Blocking

It is possible to gently shape waistlines with careful blocking—simply contract the stitches widthwise along the waist and pull them out gently at the bust and hips.

There's a lot of truth in the adage "it all comes out in the wash!" Proper finishing is essential for Fair Isle knitting. A gentle wash and careful blocking will get rid of minor stitch irregularities and smooth out the surface. If you've used Shetland (or a Shetland-type) wool, the yarn will fluff up and "bloom" to create the characteristic "halo" of fibers over the entire surface that results in a beautifully subtle blending of all the colors.

Wash your knitting in lukewarm water with a mild soap, squeezing gently but never agitating. Let the piece soak for at least fifteen minutes to ensure the yarn is wet all the way to its core. Rinse thoroughly with water of the same temperature, then gently squeeze out the water, being careful not to twist or wring the knitting. Finally, roll the piece in an absorbent towel to extract as much moisture as possible.

At this point, the piece will be amazingly elastic and you'll be able to shape it into just the size you want. Place it on a blocking board or a flat surface such as a rug or

firm bed that's been covered with a clean towel. Using rustproof T-pins, carefully pin the piece to the dimensions given in the schematic, if there is one. To maintain the elasticity of ribbing, do not block ribbed areas. Allow the piece to air-dry thoroughly before moving it. If the ribbing does inadvertently stretch, wet just the ribbing, contract it as much as possible, then allow it to air-dry thoroughly.

Fair Isle garments are traditionally stretched and dried on woolly boards—garment-shaped frames that are slightly larger than the knitted piece. You can make your own woolly board by cutting a piece of thick cardboard or foamcore to the desired measurements. Insert the form into the damp garment and allow the garment to air-dry thoroughly before removing the form.

On Your Own

You should now have all the tools you need to continue the fine tradition of Fair Isle knitting. Remember that just as real champagne only comes from Champagne, France, true Fair Isle knitting only comes from the knitters of Fair Isle. But we can all benefit from their hundreds of years of expertise in creating our own new and exciting Fair Isle styles.

Glossary of Terms and Techniques

Abbreviations

beg(s)	begin(s); beginning
bet	between
BO	bind off
CC	contrast color
cir	circular
cm	centimeter(s)
cn	cable needle
CO	cast on
cont	continue(s); continuing
dec(s)('d)	decrease(s); decreasing; decreased
dpn	double-pointed needles
foll	follow(s); following
g	gram(s)
inc(s)('d)	increase(s); increasing; increased
k	knit
k1f&b	knit into the front and back of same stitch
k2tog	knit 2 stitches together
kwise	knitwise, as if to knit
m	marker(s)

MC	main color
mm	millimeter(s)
M1	make one (increase)
oz	ounce
p	purl
p1f&b	purl into front and back of same stitch
p2tog	purl 2 stitches together
patt(s)	pattern(s)
pm	place marker
psso	pass slipped stitch over
pwise	purlwise, as if to purl
rem	remain(s); remaining
rep(s)	repeat(s); repeating
Rev St st	reverse stockinette stitch
rnd(s)	round(s)
RS	right side
sl	slip
sl st	slip st (slip 1 stitch purlwise unless otherwise indicated)

ssk	slip, slip, knit (decrease)
st(s)	stitch(es)
St st	stockinette stitch
tbl	through back loop
tog	together
WS	wrong side
wyb	with yarn in back
wyf	with yarn in front
yd	yard(s)
yo	yarnover
*	repeat starting point
* *	repeat all instructions between asterisks
( )	alternate measurements and/or instructions
[ ]	work instructions as a group a specified number of times

Bind-Offs

Standard Bind-Off

Knit the first stitch, *knit the next stitch (two stitches on right needle), insert left needle tip into first stitch on right needle (**Figure 1**) and lift this stitch up and over the second stitch (**Figure 2**) and off the needle (**Figure 3**). Repeat from * for the desired number of stitches.

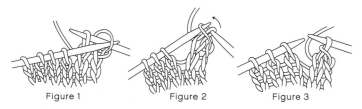

Figure 1   Figure 2   Figure 3

Three-Needle Bind-Off

Place the stitches to be joined onto two separate needles and hold the needles parallel so that the right sides of knitting face together. Insert a third needle into the first stitch on each of the two needles (**Figure 1**) and knit them together as one stitch (**Figure 2**), *knit the next stitch on each needle the same way, then use the left needle tip to lift the first stitch over the second and off the needle (**Figure 3**). Repeat from * until no stitches remain on the first two needles. Cut yarn and pull tail through last stitch to secure.

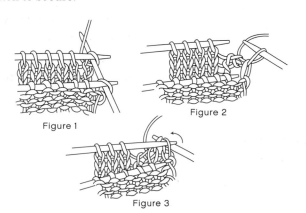

Figure 1   Figure 2

Figure 3

Blocking

Steam Blocking

Pin the pieces to be blocked to a blocking surface. Hold an iron set on the steam setting ½" (1.3 cm) above the knitted surface and direct the steam over the entire surface (except ribbing). You can get similar results by lapping wet cheesecloth on top of the knitted surface and touching it lightly with a dry iron. Lift and set down the iron gently; do not use a pushing motion.

Wet-Towel Blocking

Run a large bath or beach towel (or two towels for larger projects) through the rinse/spin cycle of a washing machine. Roll the knitted pieces in the wet towel(s), place the roll in a plastic bag, and leave overnight so that the knitted pieces become uniformly damp. Pin the damp pieces to a blocking surface and let air-dry thoroughly.

Cast-Ons

Backward-Loop Cast-On

*Loop working yarn and place it on needle backward so that it doesn't unwind. Repeat from *.

Crochet Provisional Cast-On

With waste yarn and crochet hook, make a loose crochet chain (see page 149) about four stitches more than you need to cast on. With knitting needle, working yarn, and beginning two stitches from end of chain, pick up and knit one stitch through the back loop of each crochet chain (**Figure 1**) for desired number of stitches. When you're ready to work in the opposite direction, pull out the crochet chain to expose live stitches (**Figure 2**).

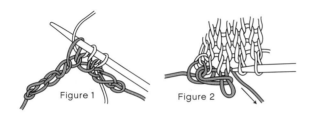

Figure 1   Figure 2

Double-Start Cast-On

Make a doubled long tail by pulling out a length of yarn needed for casting on the required number of stitches and then adding the same amount again. Fold this length in half and, with all the strands held together, make a slip-knot about 5" (12.5 cm) from the end with the cut tail, and place on a needle held in your right hand. Set up as for the long-tail method (see page 149), with the doubled yarn around your left thumb and the single yarn (attached to the ball) around your left index finger.

The slipknot counts as the first two stitches.

To make stitch A, work as for the long-tail method.

To make stitch B, remove your thumb from the double loop and reinsert it so that the yarn wraps in the opposite direction (**Figure 1**).

Bring the needle under the yarn between your index finger and thumb, then over the yarn around your index finger, and back through the thumb loop (**Figure 2**).

Drop the loop off your thumb and, placing your thumb back in the original V formation, tighten up the resulting stitch on the needle—there will be four stitches on the needle: the slipknot (counts as two stitches) and the next two stitches (A and B).

Continue to alternate stitches A and B for the desired number of stitches. The stitches will be grouped in pairs on the needle (**Figure 3**).

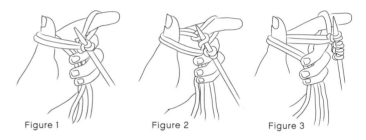

Figure 1   Figure 2   Figure 3

Knitted Cast-On

If there are no stitches on the needles, make a slipknot of working yarn and place it on the left needle. When there is at least one stitch on the left needle, *use the right needle to knit the first stitch (or slipknot) on left needle (**Figure 1**) and place new loop onto left needle to form a new stitch (**Figure 2**). Repeat from * for the desired number of stitches, always working into the last stitch made.

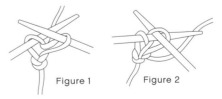

Figure 1   Figure 2

Long-Tail (Continental) Cast-On

Leaving a long tail (about ½" [1.3 cm] for each stitch to be cast on), make a slipknot and place on right needle. Place thumb and index finger of your left hand between the yarn ends so that working yarn is around your index finger and tail end is around your thumb and secure the yarn ends with your other fingers. Hold your palm upward, making a V of yarn (**Figure 1**). *Bring needle up through loop on thumb (**Figure 2**), catch first strand around index finger, and go back down through loop on thumb (**Figure 3**). Drop loop off thumb and, placing thumb back in V configuration, tighten resulting stitch on needle (**Figure 4**). Repeat from * for the desired number of stitches.

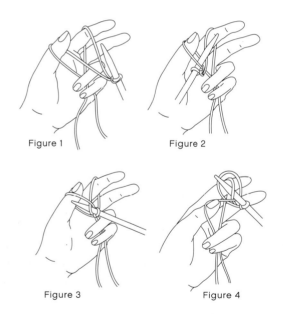

Figure 1   Figure 2

Figure 3   Figure 4

Crochet

Make a slipknot and place on crochet hook. *Yarn over hook and draw through a loop on the hook. Repeat from * for the desired number of stitches. To fasten off, cut yarn and draw end through last loop made.

Reverse Single Crochet

Working from left to right, insert hook into a stitch, draw through a loop, bring yarn over hook, and draw it through the first loop. *Insert hook into next stitch to the right (**Figure 1**), draw through a loop, bring yarn over hook again (**Figure 2**), and draw a loop through both loops on hook (**Figure 3**). Repeat from * for the desired number of stitches.

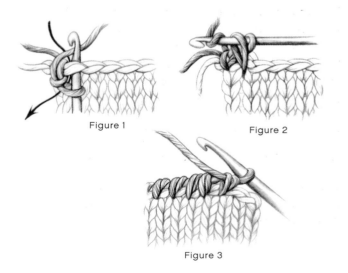

Figure 1   Figure 2

Figure 3

Decreases

Slip, Slip, Knit (ssk)

Slip two stitches individually knitwise (**Figure 1**), insert left needle tip into the front of these two slipped stitches, and use the right needle to knit them together through their back loops (**Figure 2**).

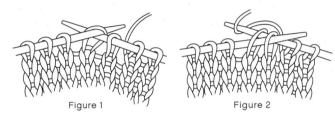

Figure 1   Figure 2

I-Cord
(also called Knit-Cord)

This is worked with two double-pointed needles. Cast on the desired number of stitches (usually three to four). Knit across these stitches, then *without turning the needle, slide stitches to other end of needle, pull the yarn around the back, and knit the stitches as usual. Repeat from * for desired length.

Embroidery

Duplicate Stitch

Bring threaded needle out from back to front at the base of the V of the knitted stitch you want to cover. *Working from right to left, pass the needle in and out under the stitch in the row above it and back into the base of the same stitch. Bring needle back out at the base of the V of the next stitch to the left. Repeat from * as desired.

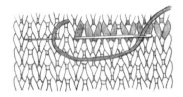

French Knot

Bring threaded needle out of knitted background from back to front, wrap yarn around needle one to three times, then use your thumb to hold the wraps in place while you insert needle into background a short distance from where it came out. Pull the needle through the wraps into the background.

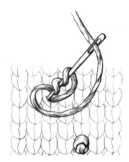

Increases
Bar Increase

KNITWISE (K1F&B)

Knit into a stitch, but leave the stitch on the left needle (**Figure 1**), then knit through the back loop of the same stitch (**Figure 2**) and slip the original stitch off the needle (**Figure 3**).

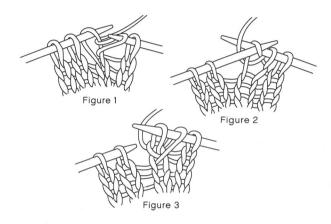

Figure 1

Figure 2

Figure 3

PURLWISE (P1F&B)

Work as for a knitwise bar increase, but purl into the front and back of the same stitch.

Raised Make-One (M1) Increase

Note: *Use the left slant if no direction of slant is specified.*

LEFT SLANT (M1L)

With left needle tip, lift the strand between the last knitted stitch and the first stitch on the left needle from front to back (**Figure 1**), then knit the lifted loop through the back (**Figure 2**).

To work this decrease purlwise (M1L pwise), purl the lifted loop through the back.

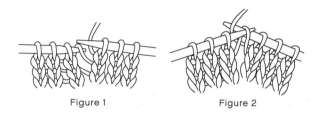

Figure 1

Figure 2

RIGHT SLANT (M1R)

With left needle tip, lift the strand between the needles from back to front (**Figure 1**). Knit the lifted loop through the front (**Figure 2**).

To work this decrease purlwise (M1R pwise), purl the lifted loop through the front.

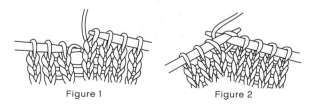

Figure 1

Figure 2

Seams

Kitchener-Stitch Grafting

Arrange stitches on two needles so that there is the same number of stitches on each needle. Hold the needles parallel to each other with wrong sides of the knitting facing together. Allowing about ½" (1.3 cm) per stitch to be grafted, thread matching yarn on a tapestry needle. Work from right to left as follows:

Step 1: Bring tapestry needle through the first stitch on the front needle as if to purl and leave the stitch on the needle (**Figure 1**).

Step 2: Bring tapestry needle through the first stitch on the back needle as if to knit and leave that stitch on the needle (**Figure 2**).

Step 3: Bring tapestry needle through the first front stitch as if to knit and slip this stitch off the needle, then bring the tapestry needle through the next front stitch as if to purl and leave this stitch on the needle (**Figure 3**).

Step 4: Bring tapestry needle through the first back stitch as if to purl and slip this stitch off the needle, then bring the tapestry needle through the next back stitch as if to knit and leave this stitch on the needle (**Figure 4**).

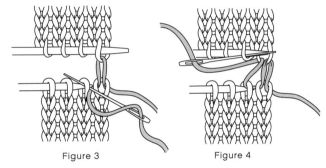

Figure 3   Figure 4

Repeat Steps 3 and 4 until one stitch remains on each needle, adjusting the tension to match the rest of the knitting as you go. To finish, bring the tapestry needle through the front stitch as if to knit and slip this stitch off the needle, then bring the tapestry needle through the back stitch as if to purl and slip this stitch off the needle.

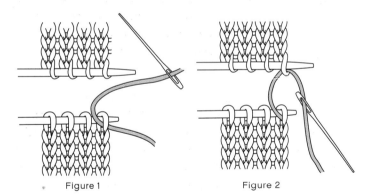

Figure 1   Figure 2

Mattress Stitch

Place the pieces to be seamed on a table, right sides facing up. Begin at the lower edge and work upward as follows:

Insert threaded needle under one bar between the two edge stitches on one piece, then under the corresponding bar plus the bar above it on the other piece (**Figure 1**). *Pick up the next two bars on the first piece (**Figure 2**), then the next two bars on the other (**Figure 3**). Repeat from *, ending by picking up the last bar or pair of bars on the first piece.

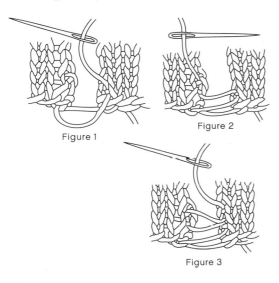

Figure 1

Figure 2

Figure 3

Running Stitch

Bring threaded needle in and out of fabric (or layers of fabric) to form a dashed line.

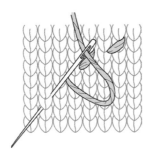

Whipstitch

Hold pieces to be sewn together so that the edges to be seamed are even with each other. With yarn threaded on a tapestry needle, *insert needle through both layers from back to front, then bring needle to back. Repeat from *, keeping even tension on the seaming yarn.

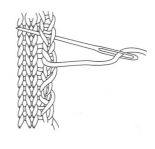

Short-Rows

Short-Rows Knit Side

Work to turning point, slip next stitch purlwise (**Figure 1**), bring the yarn to the front, then slip the same stitch back to the left needle (**Figure 2**), turn the work around and bring the yarn in position for the next stitch—one stitch has been wrapped and the yarn is correctly positioned to work the next stitch.

To hide the wrap on a subsequent knit row, work it together with the wrapped stitch as follows: Insert right needle tip under the wrap (from the front if wrapped stitch is a knit stitch [**Figure 3**]; from the back if wrapped stitch is a purl stitch) then into the stitch on the needle, and knit the stitch and its wrap together as a single stitch.

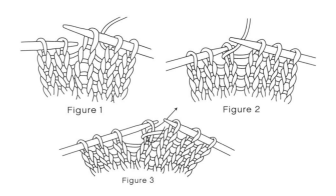

Figure 1

Figure 2

Figure 3

Short-Rows Purl Side

Work to the turning point, slip the next stitch purlwise to the right needle, bring the yarn to the back of the work (**Figure 1**), return the slipped stitch to the left needle, bring the yarn to the front between the needles (**Figure 2**), and turn the work so that the knit side is facing—one stitch has been wrapped, and the yarn is correctly positioned to knit the next stitch.

To hide the wrap on a subsequent purl row, work to the wrapped stitch, use the tip of the right needle to pick up the wrap from the back, place it on the left needle (**Figure 3**), then purl it together with the wrapped stitch.

Staystitch

Backstitch

Bring threaded needle out from back to front between the first two knitted stitches. *Insert the needle at the right edge of the right stitch, then bring it back out at the left edge of the second stitch. Insert the needle again between these two stitches and bring it out between the next two. Repeat from *.

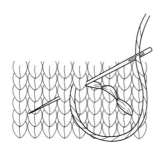

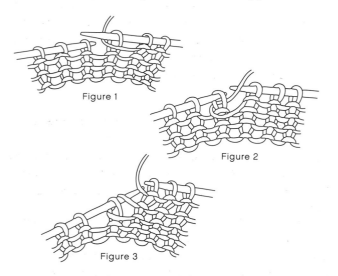

Figure 1

Figure 2

Figure 3

Contributing Designers

Elinor Brown maintains a shadow career as a knitting pattern designer while attending medical school at the Ohio State University. Elinor is an obligate knitter, and a half-knitted sleeve invariably pokes out of a pocket of her white coat. She writes about her knitting at exercisebeforeknitting.com.

Cheryl Burke hasn't stopped knitting since she picked up a pair of needles. She loves using yarn to explore color, texture, and all sorts of patterns. Her work has been published by *Twist Collective*, Berroco, and WEBS. You can find Cheryl on Ravelry.com and Flickr.com, under the username yarnbee.

Author of many books, including *Folk Knitting in Estonia* and *Knitted Lace of Estonia* (Interweave, 1999 and 2008), **Nancy Bush** has a great interest in projects with traditional stories and patterns. She teaches at home and abroad, writes books and articles, and designs from her home in Utah.

Kat Coyle knits most every day at her welcoming Los Angeles yarn shop The Little Knittery (thelittleknittery .com). She is author of *Boho Baby Knits: Groovy Patterns for Cool Tots* (Potter Craft, 2007). Her work has been published in many books and magazines, including *Lace Style*, *Simple Style*, *Knit Wit*, *Greetings from Knit Café*, *Interweave Knits*, *Knitscene*, *Twist Collective*, and *Knitty*.

Design director for Berroco, **Norah Gaughan's** designs have been featured in all major knitting periodicals and in many books. She is author of *Knitting Nature: 39 Designs Inspired by Patterns in Nature* (Stewart, Tabori and Chang, 2006), a collection inspired by fractals—complex geometric figures made up of patterns that repeat themselves at smaller and smaller, or larger and larger, scales. Catch up with Norah at blog.berroco.com.

Lucinda Guy is author of seven knitting and crochet books. She combines her love of folk art, traditional, and Scandinavian knitting techniques with authentic woolen yarns to create garments, accessories, and toys. Lucinda divides her time between researching, traveling, designing, writing, and teaching workshops. Learn more at lucindaguy.com.

Carrie Bostick Hoge is the art director and designer at Quince & Co. yarns, where she also wears hats as photographer and stylist. Her work has been featured in *Twist Collective*, *Wool People*, *Mollie Makes*, *Interweave Knits*, *Knitscene*, and at her own website, maddermade.com.

Born in the Shetland Islands, Scottish knitwear designer **Gudrun Johnston** often incorporates traditional Shetland techniques and motifs into a contemporary context. Gudrun's self-published books of patterns, *Shetland Tradebook One* and *Knit With Me: A Mother-Daughter Collection*, as well as her individual patterns, are available at yarn shops and her website, theshetlandtrader.com.

Mags Kandis has spent the past twenty years perfecting her distinct style, both as creative director of Mission Falls and for ready-to-wear manufacturers. She is author of *Folk Style* and *Gifted: Lovely Little Things to Knit and Crochet* (Interweave, 2007 and 2010). Her designs have also appeared in *Interweave Knits*, *Vogue Knitting*, *Knitter's*, and the Interweave Style book series. Find out more at MyWabiSabiCountryLife.blogspot.com.

Kirsten Kapur has been knitting for as long as she can remember. She loves to design all types of projects but is particularly drawn to colorwork. Kirsten has knitted in most of the music venues around New York City, including the now defunct CBGB while listening to her children perform. Follow Kirsten at throughtheloops.typepad.com.

Courtney Kelley is co-owner of Kelbourne Woolens, distributor of the Fibre Company unique artisan yarns. She, along with Kate Gagnon Osborn, is also coauthor of *Vintage Modern Knits* and *November Knits* (Interweave, 2011 and 2012). Her designs have appeared in *Interweave Knits*, *Interweave Crochet*, *Knitscene*, and *Vogue Knitting*.

Kate Gagnon Osborn is co-owner of Kelbourne Woolens and coauthor of *Vintage Modern Knits* and *November Knits* with Courtney Kelley. In addition to a popular line of patterns published through Kelbourne Woolens, Kate's designs have appeared in *Vogue Knitting*, *Interweave Knits*, and *Knitscene*, as well as books such as *Weekend Hats* (Interweave 2011), *Knit Local* (Sixth&Spring, 2011), *New England Knits* (Interweave 2010), and *The Best of Knitscene* (Interweave, 2011).

From her home in the hilly Piedmont of North Carolina, **Lisa Shroyer** works as editor of *Interweave Knits* magazine. Her second sweater ever was a pattern from Ann Feitelson's *The Art of Fair Isle Knitting* (Interweave, 1996)—and that's how she got hooked on colorwork. Lisa is author of *Knitting Plus: Mastering Fit + Plus-Size Style + 15 Projects* (Interweave, 2011).

SpillyJane, otherwise known as **Jane Dupuis,** lives and knits in a century-old house in Windsor, Ontario, with her husband and stuffed pheasant, Phileas. She has an unnatural affection for both mittens and socks. Visit her blog at spillyjane.blogspot.com.

When she's not knitting, **Elli Stubenrauch** enjoys genealogical research, organizing, and playing the cello her father built for her. Her knitting patterns have been featured in many books, including *Knit Local* (Sixth&Spring, 2011), *Stitch & Bitch Superstar Knitting* (Workman, 2010), and *November Knits* (Interweave, 2012). Find out more at elliphantom.com.

Scottish designer **Ysolda Teague** is the author of the pattern collection and resource book *Little Red in the City* (Ysolda Teague, 2011), three books in her Whimsical Little Knits series, and *Saturday Treat*. She has many patterns published in *Twist Collective* and *Knitty*. Her many other patterns are available on her website (ysolda.com) and in yarn stores.

Bibliography

Allen, Pam and Ann Budd. *Color Style: Innovative to Traditional, 17 Inspired Designs to Knit.* Loveland, Colorado: Interweave, 2008.

Bush, Nancy. *Folk Socks: The History & Techniques of Handknitted Footwear.* Loveland, Colorado: Interweave, 1994; updated edition, 2012.

Don, Sarah. *Fair Isle Knitting.* Mineola, New York: Dover Publications, 2007.

Feitelson, Ann. *The Art of Fair Isle Knitting: History, Technique, Color & Patterns.* Loveland, Colorado: Interweave, 1996; updated edition, 2009.

Huff, Mary Scott. *The New Stranded Colorwork: Techniques & Patterns for Vibrant Knitwear.* Loveland, Colorado: Interweave, 2009.

McGregor, Sheila. *The Complete Book of Traditional Fair Isle Knitting.* Mineola, New York: Dover Publications, 2003.

Mucklestone, Mary Jane. *200 Fair Isle Motifs: A Knitter's Directory.* Loveland, Colorado: Interweave, 2011.

Pearson, Michael. *Michael Pearson's Traditional Knitting.* New York: Van Nostrand Reinhold Co. Inc., 1984. Revised edition scheduled in 2013 by Dover.

Radcliffe, Margaret. *The Essential Guide to Color Knitting Techniques.* North Adams, Massachusetts: Storey Publishing, 2008.

Rutt, Richard. *A History of Hand Knitting.* Loveland, Colorado: Interweave, 1989.

Smith, Mary. *A Shetland Knitter's Notebook.* Lerwick, Shetland: The Shetland Times Ltd., 1991.

Smith, Mary and Maggie Liddle. *A Shetland Pattern Book.* Lerwick, Shetland: The Shetland Times Ltd., 1992.

Starmore, Alice. *Alice Starmore's Book of Fair Isle Knitting.* Mineola, New York: Dover Publications, 2009.

Swansen, Meg and Amy Detjen. *Knitting with Two Colors: Techniques for Stranded Knitting and Designing Color-Patterned Garments.* Pittsville, Wisconsin: Schoolhouse Press, 2011.

Sources for Yarns

Berroco Inc.
1 Tupperware Dr., Ste. 4
North Smithfield, RI 02896
berroco.com

Brooklyn Tweed
34 Danforth St., Ste. 110
Portland, ME 04101
brooklyntweed.net

Brown Sheep Company
100662 County Rd. 16
Mitchell, NE 69357
brownsheep.com

Cascade Yarns
PO Box 58168
1224 Andover Park E.
Tukwila, WA 98188
cascadeyarns.com

Classic Elite Yarns
16 Esquire Rd., Unit 2
North Billerica, MA 01862
classiceliteyarns.com

Elemental Affects
17555 Bubbling Wells Rd.
Desert Hot Springs, CA
92241
elementalaffects.com

Green Mountain Spinnery
PO Box 568
Putney, VT 05346
spinnery.com

Harrisville Designs
Center Village
PO Box 806
Harrisville, NH 03450
harrisville.com

Jamieson & Smith
90 North Rd.
Lerwick, Shetland
ZE1 0PQ
shetlandwoolbrokers
.co.uk

**Kelbourne Woolens/
The Fibre Company**
2000 Manor Rd.
Conshohocken, PA 19428
kelbournewoolens.com

Quince and Company
85 York St.
Portland, ME 04101
quinceandco.com

**Simply Shetland/
Jamieson's of Shetland**
18375 Olympic Ave. S.
Seattle, WA 98188
simplyshetland.net

Sunday Knits
240 Lovesee Rd.
Roscoe, IL 61073
sundayknits.com

St-Denis
stdenisyarns.com

Tutto Santa Fe/Isager
218 Galisteo St.
Santa Fe, NM 87501
tuttosantafe.com

Index

abbreviations 146
analogous color 139

backstitch 154
backward-loop cast-on 147
bar increase 151
bind-offs 147
blocking 145, 147

cast-ons 65, 147–149
charts, reading 133–134
circular knitting 134
color 139–143; changing
    131; choosing 140–143;
    combining 140–143
color placement 142–143
color dominance 128
color swatching 143–144
complementary color 139
Continental cast-on 149
crochet chain 149
crochet provisional cast-
    on 148
crochet, reverse single 149;
    slip-stitch 137
closed-loop cast-on 65

decreases 150
double-start cast-on 148
duplicate stitch 150

embroidery stitches 150

ends, weaving in 144

finishing 144–145
floats 129–130; preventing
    long 130
French knot 150

gauge 135–136
grafting 152

holding yarn 128–129
hue 139

I-cord 150
increases 151

join, jogless 134

Kitchener stitch 152
knit-cord 150
knit 1 front and back
    (k1f&b) 151
knitted cast-on 148

long-tail cast-on 149

mattress stitch 153
mistakes, correcting
    144–145
motifs 138; marking 133

patterns, choosing 138–139

peerie patterns 138
purl 1 front and back
    (p1f&b) 151

raised make-one increase
    (M1) 151
running stitch 153

seams 152–153
shade, color 139
Shetland wool 131
short-rows 153–154
slip, slip, knit (ssk) 150
slip-stitch crochet 137
staystitch 137, 154
steeks 136–137
swatch, color 143–144;
    gauge 135–136

three-needle bind-off 147
tint 139
tone 139

yarn, changing 131; choos-
    ing 131; holding 128–129;
    "sticky" 129, 131, 132;
    weights 132
yarns 131–132
yarn tooth 131

whipstitch 153
wool 129, 131

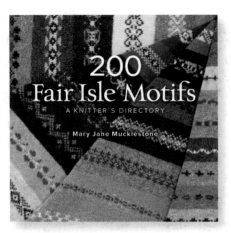